Neverending Wars

Neverending Wars:

The International Community, Weak States, and the Perpetuation of Civil War

ANN HIRONAKA

HARVARD UNIVERSITY PRESS

Cambridge, Massachusetts
London, England

Library of Congress Cataloging-in-Publication Data

Hironaka, Ann.

Neverending wars : the international community, weak states, and the
perpetuation of civil war / Ann Hironaka.

    p.   cm.

Includes bibliographical references and index.

ISBN 0-674-01532-0 (alk. paper)

1. Civil war—Developing countries.   2. Ethnic conflict—Developing
countries.   3. Intervention (International law)   4. International relations.
I. Title: Neverending wars.   II. Title.

JZ6385.H57 2005
303.6'4'091724—dc22   2004052600

To Evan, with love and gratitude

Acknowledgments

THIS BOOK BEGAN as a straightforward empirical investigation into the causes of the increased duration of civil war. Thanks to the kind encouragement and intellectual support of colleagues, the argument has expanded into a comprehensive picture of the changed nature of contemporary civil wars. Recent events have created an urgent need for such an account of civil war and intervention.

I would particularly like to thank John Meyer and Lynn Eden, who provided substantial encouragement and feedback at critical moments. I also thank Fiona Adamson, Ron Aminzade, Aaron Belkin, John Boli, Elizabeth Boyle, Frank Dobbin, Tanisha Fazal, Pamela Feldman, David John Frank, Joe Galaskiewicz, Ron Hassner, Susan Olzak, Francisco Ramirez, Joachim Savelsberg, Teresa Swartz, Marc Ventresca, and members of the Stanford Comparative Workshop. All of these scholars read chapters and provided invaluable insights and encouragement. I would also like to thank James Fearon for generously making his working papers available to me. Daniel Chirot and Ronald Jepperson offered much needed comments, corrections, and support. Michael Aronson, the editor at Harvard University Press, gave me encouragement throughout the process. Much of this work was funded by a Spencer Foundation fellowship from the National Academy of Education. And I would especially like to thank Evan Schofer for his support and also for his extensive editing, without which this book would be much less comprehensible.

Contents

Neverending Wars

1

The International Ecology of Civil Wars

CIVIL WAR HAS BECOME A way of life in some countries. In Angola two generations have grown up under conditions of civil war; they "have never lived in conditions of peace and stability and do not know what [the] peaceful development of the state is about" (Fituni 1995:147). Decades-long civil wars were unfortunately all too common in the latter half of the twentieth century and continue into the twenty-first. Countries such as Angola and Myanmar have experienced civil wars lasting their entire history as independent states. Other countries, such as the Philippines, Sri Lanka, and the Sudan have been embroiled in seemingly intractable civil wars throughout much of their history. These lengthy civil wars are a distinctive feature of the post–World War II era. In the first half of the twentieth century (and earlier), civil wars tended to be short and decisive. From 1900 to 1944, the length of the average civil war was just one and a half years. By the second half of the twentieth century, the average civil war had tripled in length, last-ing over four years, while several have lasted for decades (as calculated from the Correlates of War civil wars dataset). Moreover, the figure of four years is deceptively low, as some of the "short" wars were arguably part of longer conflicts that temporarily ebbed only to recur in later years.

These civil wars have been enormously costly in terms of human suf-fering. Sadly, the lengthening of civil wars has not been accompanied

1

by a decline in their intensity. Quite the opposite, lengthy civil wars are typically fierce conflicts with very high casualties. In Angola, it is estimated that nearly 10 percent of the population was killed by civil conflict since independence (Sivard 1996). Taken all together, civil wars since 1945 have killed over 25 million people, and millions more have become homeless or have fled as refugees (Sivard 1996; Saideman 2001). The economies of entire countries have collapsed under the burden of civil war. Myanmar (Burma), once considered one of the more prosperous of the British colonies, recently had to request the United Nations to downgrade its status to "least developed country," given the debilitating effect of nearly thirty years of civil war (Arnold 1991:475). Uganda and Angola had similarly promising prospects for development before catastrophic civil wars decimated their economies and forced them into poverty.

I propose to explain this dramatic historical increase in the length of civil wars by emphasizing changes in the international system that have literally transformed the type of states that exist in the world. In the eighteenth century, the Western world was made up of a relatively small number of strong states whose borders shifted frequently. In contrast, the contemporary period sees many more states—often very weak ones—whose borders are typically stable. This has been brought about by shifts in the climate of the international system that encouraged the breakup of the colonial empires and promoted the independence of former colonies. Many of the states that became independent after World War II lacked the resources and governmental capacity of their older, more established counterparts. The international system has generally backed these new states, providing economic support and even military protection at times. Although this policy has allowed these weak states to maintain their borders and sovereignty, it has also contributed to their domestic instability in a number of ways. In addition to international respect of territorial integrity, the Cold War and a historical context encouraging interstate military intervention in the post-1945 era have exacerbated civil strife within these weak states.

I seek to explain the increased duration of civil wars, not the original causes. The initial sources of civil conflict are often rooted in local issues and circumstances. Once a civil war has begun, however, international processes play a critical role in perpetuating the conflict and even escalating the intensity of the war. As Charles Tilly has persuasively argued, grievances are universal (Snyder and Tilly 1972). Regardless of the intensity of the grievance, however, few groups acting alone have access to sufficient resources to wage large-scale civil war over long periods of time. My aim is to examine the international processes that enable local grievances to develop into a lengthy civil war—not to explain the formation of the grievances in the first place.

The argument developed in this book addresses civil war—large-scale, organized, and sustained conflict between a state and domestic political actors. This definition excludes one-sided violence, such as a state massacre of civilians. In addition, civil wars are defined as high-intensity conflicts. They involve major casualties and significant amounts of resources, in contrast to less deadly forms of social conflict such as riots or social movements. The Correlates of War dataset, the main source of statistical data used in this study, classifies civil wars as conflicts in which over a thousand war-related casualties occur per year of conflict. This may not seem like many casualties—especially when one considers that civil wars in Mozambique, Nigeria, Sudan, Cambodia, and elsewhere have exceeded one million casualties. Fortunately, only a few civil wars resulted in such losses. Based on the 1,000 casualty-per-year criterion, there were 104 civil wars between 1944 and 1997, and 213 total in the period from 1816 to 1997 (Sarkees 2000). It should be noted that several civil conflicts that have garnered much attention among Western scholars and the Western media fail to meet this criterion. For instance, the conflict in Northern Ireland and the anti-apartheid movement in South Africa did not generate that magnitude of casualties: Northern Ireland averaged around 100 casualties per year. This is not to say that such conflicts are unimportant or inconsequential. However, the focus here is on conflicts that pass a much higher casualty threshold.

Figure 1.1 displays historical trends in civil war activity since 1816. The dashed line represents the number of new civil wars that broke out in each year (averaged per decade, and smoothed to make temporal trends more visible). The graph indicates that the number of new civil wars is fairly stable over time. There is a lull in new civil wars in the late nineteenth century and a slight increase in new conflicts in the post-World War II period. But these shifts are relatively small. In some sense, the slight increase in new civil wars since 1945 is only to be expected, as

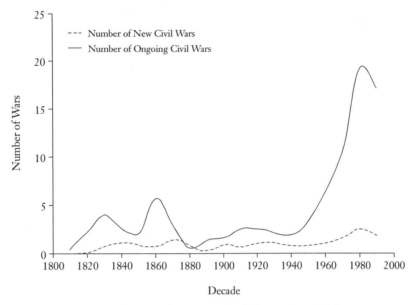

Figure 1.1 Number of New and Ongoing Civil Wars, 1816–1997

new states came into being in that period, increasing the potential sites for civil wars to occur.

A much more dramatic shift can be seen in the number of *ongoing* civil wars. The solid line in Figure 1.1 indicates the total number of ongoing civil wars being fought anywhere in the world over the period 1816–1997. Again, the line reflects the decade average, and is smoothed to make trends more apparent. Here a massive and historically unprecedented pattern emerges: the number of ongoing civil wars in the world grows tremendously following World War II. By the 1990s, roughly twenty civil wars were ongoing in the average year. This is approximately ten times the historical average, and reflects a massive new trend in conflict in the modern world.

The fact that *ongoing* wars grow more than *new* wars has only one interpretation: civil wars last much longer than they used to. Figure 1.1 provides clear evidence that civil wars begun after 1945 are of longer duration than civil wars begun earlier. The swelling of ongoing civil wars that occurs towards the end of the century represents a process of accrual. As civil wars get longer, they begin to overlap in time with each other such that there are more total wars in the world at any given moment. A civil war begins in the Philippines in 1972, for instance, and continues for more than twenty years. Another civil war begins in Angola in 1975, and also continues to the end of the century. Civil wars begin in different years, but since many continue for over a decade, they add up to many ongoing civil wars by the 1990s.

The large number of ongoing civil wars in 1997, therefore, represents the continuation of civil wars begun several years, even decades, previously. Observers of the post-Cold War world have erroneously attributed the growth of civil wars around the world to an explosion of ethnic conflict enabled by the fall of communism. Figure 1.1 suggests a different interpretation. There was no "explosion" of new civil wars after the end of the Cold War: most of the civil wars recorded in 1990 had begun in the 1970s and early 1980s, when the Cold War was in full swing. Indeed, the end of the Cold War actually led to a decrease in civil wars, as those civil wars associated with the Cold War ended within a few years of the fall of the Soviet Union (see Chapter 5).

In sum, Figure 1.1 provides information on the total number of civil wars occurring in the world and suggests that civil wars have lengthened over time. It does not, however, provide information on what kind of states are experiencing those civil wars. Figure 1.2 separates wars occurring in recently independent states from those occurring in states that had been established in previous centuries. In the nineteenth century, the recently independent states are mainly found in Latin America, while those of the twentieth century are mostly the postcolonial states of Africa and Asia.

Figure 1.2 shows that much of the postwar increase in ongoing civil wars is attributable to the substantial increase of civil wars in recently independent states, rather than in more established states. The dashed line shows the number of ongoing civil wars in recently independent states, which increases dramatically after 1945. In part, this increase is due to a surge in the number of newly independent states created from the breakup of the colonial empires. However, as I will argue, states that became independent in the late twentieth century were also more vulnerable to lengthy civil wars than were states established in earlier periods. The total number of ongoing civil wars is also shown in the graph. As one can see, the overall expansion of civil wars is largely due to the sudden spike in wars in recently independent nations.

THIS BOOK offers an explanation for the increasing length of civil wars. Civil wars have changed and lengthened as the international state system and states themselves have undergone fundamental changes.

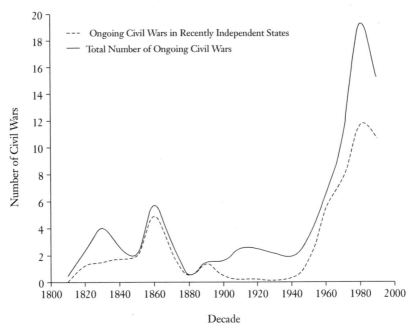

Figure 1.2 Ongoing Civil Wars in Recently Independent States, 1816–1997

In particular, there has been a deep-seated change in the way in which states are formed. In the seventeenth and eighteenth centuries, interstate warfare was frequent and intense. Charles Tilly has famously summed up the processes of state-building in early modern Europe in his aphorism: "War made the state, and the state made war" (Tilly 1975:42). As he suggests, strong states—strong in terms of resources and bureaucratic governance—were the result of the predatory character of the European state system.

This account of European state formation suggests that in those days any sufficiently strong entity could become a state, and conversely, any state that was too weak was likely to cease being a state. In that international climate, states that were unable to hold out against their militarily more powerful neighbors were in danger of losing large pieces of territory, or even their existence. Poland disappeared as a state by the late eighteenth century after being repeatedly carved up by Russia, Austria, and Prussia, and Germany and Italy arose as nation-states in large part as the result of wars in which Prussia and Sardinia forcibly unified their fellow city-states (Clodfelter 1992). As Theda Skocpol (1979) has argued persuasively, revolutions occurred mainly when domestic challenges to the state were bolstered by significant international challenges to the state.

After 1945, however, the rules and behavior changed. If one considers the international system as promoting a particular ecology of states, the population of states before 1945 was composed mostly of strong, battle-scarred states that had proven their capability to withstand both interstate and civil war. Since 1945, most colonies have achieved independence and sovereign statehood not through victory in war, but through the encouragement and support of the international system. Furthermore, international norms and laws increasingly discouraged territorial reshuffling through wars of annexation or secession. In the post-1945 era, shifting territorial boundaries became the exception rather than the rule. In a sense, the international system has locked the problems of states into specific territorial arrangements and perversely created conditions that encourage lengthy civil wars in recently independent states.

The international system after 1945 has encouraged and supported the proliferation of weak states that are susceptible to protracted civil wars. Conventional explanations of civil war often fail to perceive the substantial influence of international influences in the creation and maintenance of war-prone states. Instead, scholars typically begin with the assumption that the world's new states are fundamentally similar to older nations and focus on the specific details of different civil wars. Yet by overlooking the general processes by which states are created, these analyses fail to explain why certain states are so unstable—and thus fail to explain why certain civil wars are so intractable.

Previous Research on Civil War

Until recently, the study of civil war meant the close historical analysis of particular wars (such as the American Civil War), rather than the study of general processes that encourage or prolong them. Scholars sought to understand every minute process—the influence of individual leaders, particular government policies, or the configurations of social cleavages that promoted a particular conflict, along with many other factors. This close scrutiny provided excellent information in particular cases, but has obscured shifts in the broad trends and commonalities of civil wars.

Scholarly attention is only beginning to turn to the puzzle of the increased duration of civil wars. Three general explanations have been put forth to account for protracted wars: failure of peace negotiations and lack of trust, availability of resources to rebel groups, and ethnicity.

One argument is that civil wars continue because conflicting parties are unable to trust each other sufficiently to negotiate the termination of the war. Scholars have found that negotiations are more successful when each side can be trusted to keep the bargains it strikes (Walter 2002; Stedman et al. 2002; Fearon and Laitin 1996). In the absence of trust or third parties that can enforce compliance, negotiations frequently break down and civil wars continue. This explanation makes intuitive sense but begs the question: why is trust so hard to achieve in the contemporary period? Why were civil wars so much shorter in the first half of the twentieth century? It seems difficult to believe that human nature has changed and that people are simply less trusting today than in earlier historical periods.

Broader sociopolitical changes in the international system help to account for this long-term change. My arguments suggest that parties involved in negotiations in strong states will be more likely to trust in governmental promises than parties in weak states, because strong states have greater capacities and resources to keep their word. Additionally, civil wars that have not attracted interstate intervention or Cold War attention might have more trustworthy negotiation processes than wars in which international participants are involved, as these are beyond the control of the state that experiences the civil war.

A second explanation attributes prolonged civil war to the resources available to rebel groups. This argument was first articulated by sociologists as "resource mobilization theory" to explain social movements, but has been generalized to include revolutions and civil wars (Tilly 1975). Large-scale social movements and conflict can only occur when groups are successfully able to mobilize resources to oppose the state. Fearon and Laitin (2003) articulate variants of this argument. To begin with, great asymmetry in resources between the state and rebellious groups results in short wars. Wars do not last long when states are strong and rebels are weak (or vice versa). Conversely, the presence of "contraband" prolongs civil wars. "Contraband" refers to lucrative resources, such as opium, cocaine, or diamonds, which rebel groups can use to finance a war. In the absence of contraband, rebel resources are quickly exhausted and wars end.

I agree that resources play a central role in the maintenance of civil wars, but seek to answer a larger question: what has changed since 1945 that has allowed rebel groups to have greater parity in resources, allowing longer wars? After all, contraband in the form of diamonds or other resources was valuable and available in the first half of the century, yet civil wars in that period tended to end fairly quickly. I consider a variety of processes, such as the proliferation of weak states that cannot control their borders to prevent the flow of contraband, and third-party intervention in civil wars, which can account for the increased duration of civil wars since 1945.

A third argument attributes protracted civil war to ethnic differences. Crude versions of this argument are common in the media and public discourse. Conflicts in the Balkans, Rwanda, and elsewhere are often blamed on seething and irrational hatreds on the part of particular ethnic groups. The uniquely cohesive nature of ethnic identity is central to explanations of protracted war. Ethnic ties, it is claimed, are stronger, more rigid, and more durable than the social ties in ordinary social or political groups (Saideman 1997; Kaufmann 1996; Vanhanen 1999). Consequently, ethnic combatants are more committed than other groups and less likely to give up arms or make negotiated concessions that would allow the resolution of a civil war. Fearon and Laitin (2003) show, for instance, that civil wars involving "sons of the soil" last longer, defining "sons of the soil" as minority ethnic groups that rebel against the dominant ethnic group in power.

Here I depart sharply from the work of other scholars and theorists. I argue that while participants in many civil wars are ethnic groups, their participation does not straightforwardly explain the length, or even the original causes, of the conflict (see Chapter 4). Many ethnic or identity-based civil wars are not very different from the wars fought by other kinds of social groups (for instance, political parties, class-based groups, or regional groups). Scholars of "ethnic conflict" have not noticed this because they begin with the assumption that ethnic wars are distinctive and must be studied as a special kind of conflict. As one political scientist criticizes: "Too often, scholars seem to implicitly accept the argument that cultural or ethnic differences are at the heart of these ethnic conflicts" (Henderson 1997:650). I consider instead a variety of other factors that may explain the length of ethnic civil wars, such as the effects of state structure, Cold War factors, and interstate intervention.

While I respond to prior work on civil war, my arguments are mainly rooted in analyses that have not previously been applied to the study of civil war. The core argument builds on ideas from sociological neo-institutional theory. In addition, I draw upon several lines of research regarding the development and character of modern states and the rise of weak states in the contemporary period. Finally, I look to the political science literature on the Cold War and interstate intervention to develop several important mechanisms. These intellectual debts are clarified as I develop the central argument, below.

Neo-Institutional Perspectives on the State

The arguments developed in this book are based upon the framework of sociological neo-institutionalism. This theory highlights the influence of international structures and culture on state behavior (Meyer et al. 1997; Finnemore 1996; Jepperson, Wendt and Katzenstein 1996; Dobbin 1994; Soysal 1994; Thomas et al. 1987). Similar ideas appear in political science under the heading of "constructivism," although this tradition is associated with normative, meta-methodological, and philosophical tenets that are not part of the sociological line of thought.

The world polity refers to institutions and participants in the international sphere, including nation-state governments, intergovernmental and nongovernmental organizations, epistemic communities, diplomats, and even individuals. As a body, these actors and structures sustain and transmit ideas, discourse, norms, and shared understandings regarding models of the state and proper state behavior. Empirical research has shown that the world polity dramatically affects the structure and behavior of nation-states around the world (see Meyer et al. 1997 for a review). This may seem surprising, as the institutions, structures, and culture of the world polity possess little direct coercive power, and world norms are often violated. Yet the cultural models and taken-for-granted understandings promulgated by the world polity are quite persistent and pervasive in their slow penetration of nations, often resulting in the eventual generation of substantial social change (Schofer and Hironaka forthcoming).

I will focus on three ways in which the world polity affects states and their civil wars. First, the world polity plays a fundamental role in defining the set of states in the world, conferring statehood on some types of entities and not others (McNeely 1995). Second, the world polity sustains models of appropriate state structure that are taken for granted and widely adopted by states. Third, the world polity diffuses cultural scripts that inform and guide state behavior (Meyer et al. 1997).

The first point is perhaps the least intuitive. Scholars and the general public alike tend to take the state as given, without questioning the role of states as the fundamental actors in the international system. As political scientist Joel Migdal (2001:140) writes: "Embassies and ambassadors, the United Nations and the World Bank, foreign aid and international agencies—all implicitly or explicitly have designated the state as the proper representation of the people in a given state." Neo-institutional scholars, however, have argued that the very status of statehood is both defined and conferred collectively by the international community (McNeely 1995).

Furthermore, the idea of the state is supported by organizational structures and the recognition of statehood by the international community. States are defined as legitimate actors in international politics whereas other groups, such as secessionist sub-regions, displaced governments, or colonies, are not. The legitimacy of statehood is underscored by the acceptance of the fiction that all states are accorded equal sovereign status within the international system. This putative equality among sovereign states does not reflect the empirical differences between states in their interstate coercive power or in their intrastate ability to fulfill their function as states. Instead, the international system recognizes all states as legally equal, regardless of actual power differences.

When territories are formally recognized by the international system—even weak and disorganized territories that can barely be called "states"—they gain a great deal of legitimacy and support. External recognition confers status upon leaders, paves the way for large sums of international development aid, and provides protections via international laws and norms discouraging territorial war and annexation. Conversely, lack of recognition often spells doom for territories. The secessionist movement in the Nigerian region of Biafra in the late 1960s, for instance, gained *de facto* autonomy and arguably had the potential capacity to form an independent state. But because it was never widely recognized by the international community, its opportunities for aid were limited, and it received no international protection from continued attempts by the Nigerian state to retake the territory. The importance of international recognition becomes clear when one considers that political entities far weaker than Biafra have been accorded the status of "sovereign state" in the post-1945 era.

A second component of neo-institutional theory argues that states conform to world-level models, which provide blueprints for the features and structures of a state (Meyer et al. 1997; Thomas et al. 1987). This has generated a remarkable similarity in the structure of states—indeed, far more similarity than one would expect if states had developed autonomously from local cultures, economic systems, and historical trajectories. Instead, states all tend to address a similar set of agendas in surprisingly similar ways.

The influence of these blueprints is particularly strong in states that were formerly colonies. One reason is that the transition from colony to state was often very abrupt. Structures of governance did not evolve slowly in adaptation to local cultures and contexts. Rather, the hasty attempt to form governments often involved the wholesale importation of Western-style governance practices. These weak states were eager to adopt the trappings of modern Western states, which made them seem more legitimate in the eyes of domestic and external actors. In contrast, the developed states of Europe and North America were able to rely to a greater extent upon domestic resources and organizational capacities in the development of their state structures—although the world polity has influenced them in important ways as well.

Although states are organized around a common set of blueprints or models, weak states often lack the capacity to carry out these world-level models effectively. In most cases, the disparity between world-level model and empirical reality is due not to a lack of commitment, but to weaknesses in the organizational capacity of the state. Weak "quasi-states" lack the bureaucratic mechanisms necessary to carry out effectively the policies mandated by world-level models (Jackson and Rosberg 1982). Rather than give up, states often pursue unrealistic policies that seem hypocritical in light of empirical realities. As John

Meyer and his colleagues point out: "Decoupling [between state policies and actual practices] is endemic because nation-states are modeled on an external culture that simply cannot be imported wholesale as a fully functioning system" (Meyer et al. 1997:154).

Ironically, the attempts of weak independent states to implement these blueprints have led to conditions that foster civil war. Newly independent states develop their state structures and policies in light of what world polity blueprints dictate they *ought* to be doing, rather than focus on what they are *capable* of doing. This leads weak states to present the appearance of fully functioning states, often with up-to-date environmental standards or human rights policies, but they lack fundamental infrastructures for effective governance or containment of civil war. This fundamental weakness in state structures provides the conditions that enable protracted civil wars.

Another emphasis of neo-institutional theory is its attention to global culture, cognitive models, and ideologies that affect state behavior. States rely upon cognitive frameworks that are stored and sustained by the world polity and provide interpretations of the nature of the international system and appropriate state interests within that system. These frameworks constitute circumscribed cognitive boundaries within which rational planning and decision-making take place (March and Olsen 1984). Moreover, these frameworks tend to be "taken for granted," such that states often act upon them without reflection.

For instance, the Cold War framework regarding the meaning of capitalism and communism influenced superpower interpretations of events and sustained a set of polarized identities. Ideologies of communism and pro-Western capitalism were fundamentally rooted at the global level and had impacts substantially beyond the material resources provided by the superpowers and other interested actors. In the context of the Cold War, group identification with either communism or pro-Western capitalism had a profoundly polarizing effect— sufficient to justify all-out wars to dislodge the other. International actors, especially the superpowers, interpreted world events according to these frameworks, frequently deciding on military aid and intervention that fueled further conflict. In other words, common cultural frames polarized political activity at the national level, encouraged conflict, and rendered civil wars more intractable than they otherwise might have been.

While this study is rooted in basic ideas of neo-institutional theory, it nevertheless represents a new direction for neo-institutional research. Scholars in the neo-institutional tradition have expended considerable effort to describe the definitions and models of the state and argue that these definitions and models affect state behavior. I take seriously the institutional claims of the imagined state, but extend the argument by showing that the adoption of these blueprints has led to conditions that encourage lengthy civil wars.

The International Ecology of States

The macro-social vantage point of neo-institutional theory draws attention to the ways that the world polity affects the state system at an ecological level. The particular states that populate the international system are not a collection developed by chance. International processes are deeply implicated in the creation and maintenance of these particular states. This ecology may not represent a conscious plan on the part of world polity members. Nevertheless it is the result of other, more conscious social or political agendas, such as decolonization and development aid, that were promoted by particular actors and the world polity as a whole.

Certain processes in the world polity have been particularly influential in the construction of the structures and territorial configurations of the states that became independent after World War II. In the first place, the international system has encouraged the creation of large numbers of states from the remains of the colonial empires. The decline of interstate warfare and the development of international laws against territorial annexation have prevented these recently independent states from being absorbed by their more militarily powerful neighbors. At the same time, the members of the international system have typically refused to recognize sub-regional secessionist attempts, preventing existing states from splintering into more manageable units.

By fostering colonial independence, the international system was largely responsible for the creation of large numbers of states out of former colonies (Strang 1990; Hironaka 1998). In earlier periods, colonies had been viewed as the possessions of their imperial owners. The international system only intervened in unusual circumstances, such as the reallocation of the colonies of those imperial powers that were defeated in World War I. After World War II, however, influential members of the international system, as well as the United Nations as a whole, began to take a radically different position that called, in increasingly strident declarations, for the independence of all colonies. As more former colonies became full members of the General Assembly, notions of colonial self-determination became increasingly accepted and the international momentum for colonial independence became unstoppable. Empires that spanned continents and endured for centuries were reduced to mere handfuls of islands by the mid-1970s (Fieldhouse 1973).

The hand of the international system can be seen, for example, in the creation of Angola as a sovereign state. Portugal had been one of the first colonial powers, and was one of the last to hold on to rebellious colonies. Even after the British, French, Dutch, Spanish, and Belgian empires had broken up, the Portuguese maintained their empire in Africa, grimly claiming that their colonies were part of Portugal itself and could not be separated. Substantial international pressure was exerted on Portugal to change its stance on decolonization. A number of nations, as well as the United Nations organization itself, sharply criticized Portugal's continued colonial rule and castigated it as backward, illegitimate, and even racist. The strength of international disapproval could be likened to the treatment of South Africa prior to the end of apartheid. The United Nations General Assembly even authorized military aid on behalf of colonial independence (Jackson 1990). In 1974, this international pressure against Portugal's policies manifested itself as a leading factor in the domestic overthrow of the Portuguese government (Holland 1985; Newitt 1981). In 1975, the succeeding government immediately proclaimed the independence of the three African colonies, Angola, Mozambique, and Guinea-Bissau, and the United Nations General Assembly quickly voted to grant Angola a seat in the United Nations in 1976 (Feste 1992).

International recognition brought much more than legitimacy to the fledgling independent state of Angola. In the early 1970s, annual development aid to the colony was a pittance, ranging from literally zero to a few hundred thousand dollars per year (World Bank 2000). When Angola was admitted to the United Nations, contributions of international aid jumped to nearly fifty million dollars per year, and have (with some fluctuations) grown ever since. Unsupported as a colony, the "sovereign" state of Angola receives aid that in some years exceeds twenty percent of its gross national accounts and represents more than half of all domestic capital investment (World Bank 2000). Clearly, the cognitive and material support of the international system—especially the promptness of international recognition after Portugal's withdrawal and liberality of development aid—helped create Angola and continues to sustain its very existence as an independent state.

As part of the continuity of its anticolonial policy, the world polity has protected recently independent states from the perils of territorial annexation. In more predatory eras, militarily weak states were absorbed by their more powerful neighbors, either partially or swallowed whole. Self-defense was considered not a right but a necessity for states merely to ensure their survival. Moreover, states formed from colonies had an additional reason to fear territorial annexation. Postcolonial borders reflected the arbitrary partitioning of Africa by colonial powers. Borders were drawn up without regard to the configurations of ethnic populations or even of geographic features. Scholars predicted that all of Africa would become a battlefield as recently independent states fought interstate wars in order to replace arbitrary colonial borders with more practical boundaries (Emerson 1960). These fears were not borne out.

There have been very few territorial wars since World War II (Zacher 2001; Hironaka 1998). Neither recently independent states nor more established states have pursued territorial annexation as vigorously as states in previous historical periods. Instead, nearly all the wars since 1945 have been civil wars or international interventions in civil wars. This decline in territorial warfare has been attributed to factors such as the Cold War or the changing nature of economic development (Waltz 1979; Huth 1996). However, empirical research strongly supports neo-institutional arguments, which attribute the decline in territorial warfare to the formulation of strong international laws and norms against territorial annexation (Zacher 2001; Hironaka 1998). Over the first half of the twentieth century, the cultural and political consensus in the international community had shifted. Territorial wars, which were formerly viewed as a natural and inevitable part of international relations, became increasingly viewed as aberrant among actors in the world polity. As a result, territorial aggression was likely to garner international criticism, loss of legitimacy, or diminished external aid, and even international intervention (as in the recent case of Kuwait), making it a less palatable strategy. Whatever the cause, the result has been that recently independent states have not experienced the kind of interstate warfare that forced the European states either to develop their domestic capabilities or be weeded out by more powerful neighbors.

Angola is typical of sub-Saharan African nations in that it has not been involved in a major territorial conflict since its independence. In contrast to nineteenth-century Europe, where domestic weakness invited territorial grabs, no state has annexed Angolan territory. This is all the more surprising given the politics of the region. Angola steadily intervened in the politics of its neighbor, South Africa, through its support of anti-apartheid insurgent groups. South Africa, in turn, responded by intervening heavily in the politics and civil war of Angola. Yet the militarily powerful South Africa never attempted to annex Angola, wholly or in part. Doing so would surely have drawn tremendous international criticism, further eroding the already shaky legitimacy of the apartheid regime in South Africa. Although it is difficult to speculate about the counterfactual, one might imagine that in a different international climate South Africa might well have controlled the unwanted interventions by simply annexing Angola and taking over its government completely. As South Africa is the regionally dominant military power, such a tactic arguably lay within its military capabilities. Instead, South Africa was forced to content itself with supporting the various insurgent groups in Angola and encouraging political destabilization. The postwar infrequency of territorial war has therefore helped to protect Angola, despite the substantial trans-border politics of the region.

Another important world polity influence on recently independent states has been the refusal of the international community to recognize and legitimate secession (Jackson 1990). A secessionist attempt occurs when a sub-region of an existing state declares itself to be a sovereign state. Although declarations of secession have been fairly common throughout the twentieth century, these attempts at secession have rarely succeeded in gaining formal recognition from the international community, much less the legitimacy and resources that often accompany international recognition. In order to be successful, a secessionist region must be recognized by the international community and accepted as a full-fledged member of that community. Despite gaining

control over territory, building a government, and garnering popular support, secessionist regions such as Tibet in China, Biafra in Nigeria, and Kashmir in India failed to gain international recognition of
sovereign status. Without recognition, these regions received little in
the way of aid or external support. In these cases, the central government—often supported by a great deal of external aid—has typically
been able to regain control of secessionist regions in the long run. But
it is easy to imagine rather different historical outcomes if, for instance,
Biafra had been immediately recognized and succored by central actors
and institutions in the world polity. As a point of contrast, consider that
many former colonies that are now independent states had substantially less *de facto* control over their territory than did these secessionist
regions. The international community has the power to create states
out of unstable colonies, but it has ignored more robust candidates that
are secessionist regions, and conferred sovereign status on one rather
than the other.

The refusal of the international community to recognize most secessionist regions has protected many weak states from fragmenting. At
the same time, rejection of the option of splitting has the consequence
of locking problems within fixed territorial borders. When colonial
borders were drawn, the imperial powers did not take care to ensure
that the resulting colonies would be easily governable as independent
entities. Some recently independent states, such as Nigeria or the Congo,
are faced with governing large territorial areas populated by multiple
ethnic groups, but lack essential infrastructures such as roads, transport, and communication links throughout the country. Subdividing
such weak states into smaller, more easily governable countries might
offer a solution to their problems of management, yet the international
system actively prevents the fragmentation of states.

Like many weak states, Angola has experienced at least one secessionist attempt since independence. The Cabinda region in the north-
east corner of Angola declared secession in 1975, motivated at least
in part by fears of Angola's escalating civil war (Minahan 1995; Dos
Santos 1983). In support of its secessionist attempt, Cabinda had a government, a territory, and also had some modest resources in the form of
oil wealth. Arguably, Cabinda might have been able to support itself as
a reasonably prosperous independent country. However, the international system refused to recognize Cabinda as a sovereign state or pro-

vide aid, and Angola was able to reincorporate it in subsequent years. In sum, both the initial creation and the continued existence of Angola as a state have substantially depended upon the climate of the international system. The statement made by one scholar, that "Angola's legitimacy as a unitary state is unquestioned" (Fituni 1995:154) is true only because the international system has protected the status of Angola as a state—certainly not because of Angola's fitness or military capabilities.

As the example of Angola suggests, its continued existence is not accidental, nor is it due to the inherent capability and prowess of the state. Instead, Angola is the result of international processes that fundamentally supported its independence as a sovereign state and maintained its territorial integrity throughout its existence. Angola is by no means the sole recipient of this international attention. It is a member of a cohort of recently independent states that were formed by these same processes. The addition of these states to the international community has altered the population of states, resulting in an international ecology unlike that of other historical periods, with a large proportion of weak states which are susceptible to lengthy civil wars.

Explaining Prolonged Civil Wars in Weak States

How do the creation and international support of weak states translate to lengthier civil wars? One answer is that state weakness is itself a major factor in the prolongation of civil wars. In addition, international processes related to the Cold War and an overall increase in interstate military intervention further increase the propensity for weak states to experience lengthy civil wars. These additional factors affect weak states more severely than strong ones—much as a flu epidemic disproportionately harms the weak or infirm. This analogy should not be carried too far—obviously civil war is a social phenomenon rather than a biological one. All the same, one should keep in mind that weak states are far more vulnerable to processes that prolong civil wars compared to their more robust counterparts.

In addition to the international dynamics that maintain states, various factors more directly affect the length of civil wars: (1) the effect of weak state structure itself; (2) the Cold War for much of the period; and (3) changes in the nature and frequency of interstate intervention. It is important to note that the effects compound each other: the Cold

War and interstate interventions have the most severe impact on the civil wars in states that are weaker to begin with.

Weak States

To explain civil wars, I bring together separate strands of research on the state. The first strand explains the origins and development of the European states (Tilly 1975; Poggi 1978; Bendix 1964). The second discusses the development of recently independent states, with particular emphasis on international influences (Herbst 2000; Jackson 1990; Nettl 1968). Scholars in this tradition have noted that more recently independent states were created under quite different conditions of decolonization and interstate stability, conditions that created "quasi-states" that lack the capabilities developed earlier by the European states (Jackson 1990). The third strand builds upon the other two by distinguishing between strong states, which tend to be the more established European states, and weaker states, which tend to be recently independent, less developed states (Migdal 2001, 1988; Herbst 2000).

These research traditions have not previously been used to understand civil wars, but have primarily focused on the rise of the state and its features. On reflection, however, it seems obvious that state structures must play a role in promulgating or dampening civil conflicts. By understanding the different developmental trajectories of the European states compared with the recently independent ex-colonial states, I develop insight into why a population of weak states susceptible to lengthy civil wars exists, as well as how weak state structures affect civil wars.

World polity processes resulted in the creation of a population of recently independent, often impoverished states known as weak states or "quasi-states"—states that have the trappings of statehood but lack the capabilities of the European states (Migdal 2001; Jackson and Rosberg 1982). Since the international community did not insist on self-sufficiency as a requirement for independence, many recently independent states lack the capacity for managing and benefiting from their resources that their European predecessors were forced to develop. Many are dependent upon international development aid in order to maintain even the most basic governmental capabilities.

In addition, many recently independent states have had only a short history since independence and lack bureaucratic structure and governmental experience. In contrast, the European states took decades, even centuries, to develop rationalized bureaucratic structures that were capable of governing millions of people. Recently independent states were often forced to adopt these structures overnight. Not surprisingly, the bureaucratic and governmental structures of many of these countries are fragile, easily distorted by corruption and nepotism, and prone to being overthrown.

Thus many of the states of the Third World are not able to execute the functions specified in the world-level model of the state, and this lack of governmental capability increases their vulnerability to prolonged civil war. Angola is but one of many examples of a recently independent weak state. In the case of Angola, natural resources were available at independence, in the form of oil and diamonds, which could have provided the basis for substantial economic development. Indeed in 1973, two years before independence, Angola had one of the highest average per capita incomes in sub-Saharan Africa (Fituni 1995). But nearly all of the skilled labor in the country was Portuguese, and 90 percent of the Portuguese fled the country during the instability associated with Angola's transition to independence (Minter 1994). This loss of skilled labor led to plummeting agricultural exports and the collapse of the service sector, creating a severe economic downturn (Minter 1994).

Angola was unable to resuscitate its economy, as the onset of independence did not bring peace. Instead, the war for independence immediately turned into a bloody civil war for control of the country. This civil war, which lasted with some starts and stops for at least twenty-five years, impoverished the country even more. Economic sabotage was one of the key strategies pursued by UNITA, one of the main opposition groups, with the goal of "bringing the Angolan economy to its knees" (Minter 1994:194). The civil war has been incredibly costly to Angola, and its oil wealth has been spent in providing weapons and supplies for the combatants, rather than in the creation of a sustainable economic infrastructure for the civilian population. According to a United Nations estimate, $30 billion dollars had been spent on the war in Angola from 1980 to 1988, amounting to six times its yearly GDP (Minter 1994).

Not only did Angola lack sufficient resources to develop a functioning state, it has also suffered from a lack of adequate governmental capacity, bureaucratic structures, and governmental experience. Portugal, the colonial power, had refused to prepare for Angolan independence. Instead, Portugal had imposed a top-down administrative structure in its colonies, and few native Angolans had been allowed to play any role in the colonial government prior to independence (Minter 1994). Moreover, the Portuguese had paid little attention to education in its colonies. Illiteracy rates among Angolans at independence were in excess of 90 percent, and fewer than a thousand Angolans even had a full high school education (Minter 1994). Thus Angola was even less ready for self-governance than other African nations.

Despite this lack of personnel and governmental structure, the Angolan government was immediately confronted with the multitudinous responsibilities of a modern state. The lack of communication and means of transportation outside of the capital city increased the challenges of government. Telephone lines were irregular, and the lack of literacy among civil servants made written communication nearly useless (Minter 1994). Communication problems made face-to-face visits between officials a requirement for the functioning of the government, but travel within Angola was imperiled by guerrilla attacks. The insurgents targeted civilian travelers and destroyed the railway that ran through eastern Angola (Minter 1994). In many cases, provincial capitals were only accessible by airplane or military convoy (Minter 1994).

Unfortunately, the structural weaknesses of Angola are common in many other recently independent states as well. These structural weaknesses have created the conditions that enable civil wars, once begun, to go on for years or decades. In contrast, stronger states such as Great Britain or France are able to contain their civil conflicts to a much greater extent. Though there are exceptions, strong states are typically able to limit casualties to a small fraction of those in weak state conflicts, while maintaining effective governmental control and services throughout most of their territory.

The Cold War

The Cold War was a global phenomenon. Although it was principally "waged" from 1945 to 1989 by the superpowers and their European allies, the ideologies and cultural understandings extended throughout the world. The international system and the superpowers supported frames or meanings that were used to interpret Third World states and conflicts, substantially affecting civil wars. This labeling was consequential, however, since conflicts that were considered to be part of the Cold War were likely to last longer and receive more intervention than non-Cold War conflicts.

Recently independent states were pressured to side with either pro-Western capitalists or pro-Soviet communists. This pressure was, at times, quite overt and coercive. States that did not choose sides found that they had been interpreted by the superpowers as having chosen one anyway. In some cases the interpretation of international actors differed substantially from local interpretations. That is, superpowers or other international actors labeled and interpreted Third World conflicts as rooted in Cold War rivalry, even in cases with little connection to Marxist or pro-Western ideologies. In other cases, domestic leaders strategically signaled ideological commitments (even false ones) to suit their own advantage.

In the bitter Cold War rivalry, superpowers supported "friendly" regimes and strove to undermine "hostile" ones as a matter of course—and the other superpower often countered. In the cultural context of the Cold War, such interpretations were not only possible but were well developed theoretically (the "domino theory" of the United States, for example), and straightforwardly accepted. Military aid, advisors, weapons, development aid, and even troops on occasion poured into weak states in all parts of the world. As a result, a ready stream of resources was available to *both* the central government *and* opposition groups in several weak states. These external resources were often very large compared to the domestic economies of weak states, fueling conflict on a much larger scale than would have been possible otherwise. Civil wars could go on and on—even after domestic resources were exhausted.

The worldwide availability of two competing ideologies also served to destabilize weak states at a domestic level. Capitalism and communism both offered persuasive visions of social reform, justice, and prosperity. Local opposition groups around the world seized upon these ideologies and frames to mobilize opposition movements with explicitly revolutionary aims. Separate from military resources, the Cold War provided powerful cultural/ideological resources that supported challenges to the regimes of weak states. Unfortunately, long-standing civil wars were a common result.

Again, Angola serves as a relevant example. The Cold War aspects of Angola's civil war were imposed by the superpowers and the bipolar nature of the international system, rather than arising out of domestic political configurations. The group that ended up in control of the government, the MPLA, was widely regarded as Marxist and was allied with the Soviet Union and Cuba. The United States and China supported a rival group, the FNLA, on the grounds that it was anti-Soviet. When this group lost its bid for governmental control in the late 1970s, the United States switched its support to a third group, UNITA. This support of the superpowers was by no means limited to moral support; substantial economic and military resources were also involved. By 1989, the United States was contributing over $50 million in aid to UNITA, which equaled nearly 10 percent of the entire Angolan economy (Minter 1994). The Soviet Union was estimated to have contributed $1 billion in military support to the Marxist Angolan government in 1986–87, or 20 percent of the Angolan GDP, and a total of $4 billion in the previous decade (Rothchild and Hartzell 1992).

As was typical of many Cold War conflicts, it was unclear whether the group labeled as Marxist had been born Marxist, or whether it had Marxism thrust upon it by the politics of the international system. Originally, the politics of the three groups were muddled and none was very clearly pro- or anti-Marxist. Over time, however, the group that was backed by the Soviet Union (the MPLA) developed, not surprisingly, into a pro-Marxist group while the group backed by the United States (the FNLA) developed into an anti-Marxist group. More puzzling was the U.S. support of UNITA, which claimed a socialist ideology that was more consonant with the Soviet stance or that of the Marxist MPLA government than with the ideologies of the West. In a strange configuration, UNITA's pro-Maoist and pro-black power stance led to its alliance with the unlikely bedfellows of the United States and China (Minter 1994). Some scholars argue that the U.S. support of pro-Marxist UNITA was due primarily to the desire born out of the Cold War to oppose Soviet and Cuban activities, rather than for any ideological resonance with UNITA's political goals. Furthermore, the failure of the United States to turn Angola away from Marxism in the late 1970s had become "a symbol of US humiliation and

Soviet threat for many Washington politicians who would have had difficulty finding it [Angola] on a world map," which may have provided a continuing motivation for U.S. involvement in subsequent years (Minter 1994:145).

The example of Angola suggests that Cold War histories were not objective facts of the international system, but must be examined as interpretive processes in which perceptions of weak states as pro-Western or pro-communist were developed by international actors. Weak states were particularly susceptible to such interpretations, as U.S. or Soviet understandings of local politics were likely to be simplistic and uninformed. Stronger states, on the other hand, were better able to present and interpret themselves to the superpowers more strategically. Depending on the interpretation, however, Cold War framing allowed the marshaling of resources and allies, with significant consequences for those civil wars.

Interstate Intervention in Civil Wars

I also utilize a line of investigation that focuses on interstate intervention in civil wars. The bulk of this research examines the motivations of the intervening state, and a vast body of work on international law dissects whether these motivations and rationales for intervention were legitimate (Hoffman 1996; Damrosch 1993; Bull 1986; Vincent 1974; Higgins 1972; Brownlie 1963). Thus much of the work examines the causes and effects of intervention for the intervening states, while only a handful of studies have examined the effects of intervention for the state that is the target of the civil war (Regan 2000; Pearson 1974). Their findings support my claim that interstate intervention does significantly lengthen civil wars in the post-World War II period.

Interstate intervention turns out to be a very important factor in the lengthening of civil wars in the late twentieth century. Our analytical blindness to the prevalence of intervention is the result of the collusion of the international community, which insists that all states are sovereign actors. Thus intervention is ignored despite its pervasiveness, because acknowledgment of the multiple direct and indirect forms of intervention that support weak states might undermine assumptions about their sovereign status.

Interstate intervention has, of course, been a feature of global politics since the creation of the international system itself. But the weakness of states in the post-World War II era has led to a change in the type of interventions that occur in civil wars. One of the most notable changes has been the increase in interventions that occur on both sides of the conflict. In the nineteenth century and first half of the twentieth century, intervention was typically undertaken by a Great Power, or a set of Great Powers acting in collaboration. Moreover, these interventions tended to be in support of only one side, resulting in very short civil wars. The Great Power literally overwhelmed one or the other side of the civil war conflict.

In the latter half of the twentieth century, however, intervention frequently occurred on both the government side and the opposition side of a civil war—usually by different states. One common type of two-sided intervention occurred as part of the Cold War strategy. The superpowers routinely chose to support opposite sides of a civil war, as in Angola. Nor had intervention been limited to the superpowers in this period. Former colonial powers, regional military powers, and neighboring countries have increasingly become involved in the civil wars of their fellow states.

This increase in the frequency of intervention has been encouraged by the military weaknesses of recently independent states. Weak states usually lack the resources and organization necessary to control their territorial borders, making them liable to incursions from neighboring civil or interstate wars. In some cases, regional conflicts such as those in the Middle East or Southeast Asia overflowed the borders of nearby weak states, leading to civil wars and interventions in those civil wars. In other cases, a neighboring state might intervene in a weak state as a way of attacking its own insurgents, who often hide across a border in a nearby weak state.

For instance, the Angolan civil war attracted massive amounts of intervention as a result of these processes, in addition to the already significant intervention that resulted from its role as a Cold War prize. South Africa heavily intervened in Angola's civil war as a consequence of Pretoria's attempts to control its own civil conflicts. Opposition groups against South Africa's apartheid regime, such as the African National Congress, had taken refuge in Angola and other nearby states and set up training camps (Minter 1994). Angola had also aided SWAPO guerrillas fighting for Namibian independence during the time when Namibia (then known as South West Africa) was still a colony of South Africa (Minter 1994:4). In response, South Africa retaliated by equipping and training UNITA, one of the Angolan opposition groups, and provided bases and even backup military support (Minter 1994). This substantial support provided significant resources for the continuation of the Angolan civil war (Feste 1992).

I have used Angola to illustrate how the weak structure of many recently independent states, coupled with the international climate of the Cold War and the frequency of interstate intervention, have resulted in the long-lasting civil wars of the post-World War II period. Angola is a good example because its civil war is one of the few in which all three processes are evident and, not coincidentally, also one of the longest civil wars fought during this period. However, most of the longer civil wars that have occurred since 1945 exhibit at least one or two of the processes discussed. Table 1.1 lists the fifteen lengthiest civil wars from the Correlates of War dataset that have been fought since 1945. The columns to the right indicate whether any given war was (a) fought in a

Table 1.1 The fifteen longest civil wars, 1945–1997

Country	Length of civil war (months)	Weak state?[a]	Cold War conflict?	Interstate intervention?
Philippines	246	Yes	Yes	Yes
Ethiopia	212	Yes	No	Yes
Somalia	191	Yes	No	Yes
Angola	189	Yes	Yes	Yes
Lebanon	189	Yes	No	Yes
Afghanistan	168	Yes	Yes	Yes
Peru	168	No	Yes	Yes
Sri Lanka	168 ongoing[b]	Yes	Yes	Yes
Sudan	168 ongoing[b]	No	No	Yes
Colombia	156 ongoing[b]	No	No	Yes
Ethiopia	160	Yes	No	No
Mozambique	158	Yes	No	Yes
Cambodia	156	Yes	Yes	Yes
El Salvador	153	Yes	Yes	Yes
India	144 ongoing[b]	No	No	Yes

a. For purposes of illustration, a state was considered weak if it scored below the mean on either the economic/military factor or the government capacity factor. These variables are used in the analyses in Chapter 2 as indicators of a weak state, and a description of the coding can be found in the appendix.

b. These civil wars had not ended by 1997, the last year in the Correlates of War dataset.

state with less-than-average military or governmental capabilities; (b) characterized as a Cold War conflict; or (c) intervened upon at some point by another state. More precise definitions of these variables are given in the Appendix.

As Table 1.1 shows, Angola, listed as having the fourth-lengthiest war since 1945, is by no means unique in exhibiting all three of the characteristics that lengthen war. Many of the lengthiest wars of the late twentieth century exhibit all three characteristics, and all exhibit at least one. This is not to claim that the mere possession of one of the three characteristics is sufficient to lengthen a civil war, as the influence of each factor will vary in every case, depending on the context. Yet Table 1.1 does suggest that these three characteristics are commonplace in the lengthy civil wars of this period.

Historical Changes in Civil Wars

The argument so far has dwelt upon the processes prolonging civil wars since 1945. Comparison with an earlier period provides a useful contrast. The international climate of previous historical periods differed significantly from that of the late twentieth century, leading to the formation of different kinds of states and different dynamics of civil wars. Thus even the weaker states of previous eras were not as prone to lengthy civil war as weak states are today. The weaker of the nineteenth- and early twentieth-century states typically possessed a well-developed administration and war-hardened military, which often led to decisive conflicts. Also, international interventions tended to support only one side of a conflict (often the state rather than insurgents), in contrast to the Cold War period in which the superpowers each fueled opposite sides of a civil war. As a result, those wars tended to be short and decisive, compared to the civil wars of the modern day.

The most obvious similarity in wars across historical periods is domestic weakness. During the nineteenth century, forms of weakness led to civil wars in Latin America and also in the relatively stronger states of Europe. Although these states had proved their capacity to survive interstate warfare, they nevertheless suffered from internal struggles and resource deficits. Fiscal deficits commonly plagued the governments of Europe, particularly after the expenses of the Napoleonic Wars. Problems of internal order also arose as the European governments tried to "impose order on an anarchic society, with relatively few resources at hand" (Sperber 2000:271). In other words, even the militarily strong states of Europe suffered from bouts of internal weaknesses and instability that frequently developed into civil war.

Despite these weaknesses, however, civil wars in the nineteenth century tended to be short. In most cases, the state was the clear center of political authority and the source of the most powerful domestic structure within a country. Thus nineteenth-century civil wars almost always centered on the state itself—with one group trying to wrest control of the state from another. This sharply contrasts with contemporary civil wars, in which the central government is often so weak or irrelevant that sub-regions seek to form completely separate states. The centrality of the state in nineteenth-century conflicts meant that civil wars were fairly localized and victory was decisive—making for short civil wars. In the French civil war of 1871, for instance, fighting was mostly located in Paris. When the army stepped in on the side of the government, the opposition was defeated with relative speed (Tombs 1999; Horne 1989). Whichever side controlled the capital and the army possessed overwhelming force that could quickly and decisively defeat the enemy. As Tombs (1999:14) states: "Paris was the arena in which the outcome of France's internal struggles had repeatedly been decided" because "political power had been concentrated there since . . . 1789." Revolutionary movements needed to gain control quickly, or else the war would be lost. Lengthy wars of attrition, such as the U.S. Civil War, were the exception.

The states of the eighteenth and nineteenth centuries were also aided by the lower value placed on statehood, compared to the twentieth century. In earlier times, nonstate actors could have substantial power rivaling that of states. For instance, Thomson (1994) points out that the pirates of Tripoli were accorded a kind of *de facto* sovereignty in the early nineteenth century as a consequence of their military capacity to enforce that sovereignty, despite their lack of recognition as a sovereign state. Similarly, while states such as Virginia or Massachusetts of the United States of America lacked sovereign status on their own, they had substantial economic and political autonomy with relatively little federal oversight over their affairs, making secession seem unnecessary. In contrast, statehood in the twentieth century offers substantial rewards, such as resources and legitimacy, which are not awarded to nonstate actors. Sovereign status also protects states from interstate annexation, while nonsovereign territories such as East Timor (until recently), Tibet, and Biafra have not been accorded such international protection.

Although the nineteenth century did not have a Cold War, it did have important global ideologies that prompted civil war. Again, however, important differences resulted in very different kinds of civil war. Monarchy and democracy were alternate forms of government that had supporters in most nations—leading to debate and conflict in European and Latin American states. Several civil wars were fought between monarchists and pro-democracy movements. Although neither group had the explicitly expansionist ideologies that were a main catalyst of Cold War enmities, both monarchist and democratic regimes intervened on behalf of movements in other countries. In particular, monarchists feared that democratic regimes were dangerous and unpredictable and moved to squelch fledgling democratic movements. A bipolar world never developed, however, in large part because monarchists dominated the Great Powers throughout much of the era. Powerful, decisive interventions meant that the pro-democracy civil wars of the nineteenth century were relatively short and usually decided against the democratic proponents.

Intervention did also play an important role in the civil wars of the nineteenth century. But here again there were significant differences compared to interventions of the late twentieth century. In the nineteenth century, international coordination of interventions was quite common. The Great Powers organized decisive interventions together on one or the other side of a given civil war—usually that of the incumbent regime. This brought a swift end to civil wars. As one historian puts it: "In these circumstances of weak governments and weak oppositions, the decisive factor was the fact of outside military intervention" (Sperber 2000:347). In contrast, the interventions of the twentieth century tended to lengthen civil wars by backing both sides of the conflict and providing resources and manpower to impoverished combatants that would not otherwise have had the capacity to continue fighting. One may criticize the heavy-handedness of the nineteenth-century Great Powers, especially when it came to squashing democratic movements, but one effect was to limit civil war activity in that era.

There were, of course, exceptions among nineteenth- and early twentieth-century civil wars. The U.S. Civil War was unusual in that it was fought around regional geographic identities rather than established political parties (Donald, Baker and Holt 2001). The Spanish Civil War of the late 1930s was another exception because it drew intervention on both sides. Germany, Italy, and Portugal supported Franco, who was the leader of the opposition, while the Spanish government gathered support from France and Russia (Clodfelter 1992:604–607). In the main, however, these earlier civil wars differed in substantial ways from the civil wars of today—ways that tended to make the wars of previous centuries much shorter.

To develop in greater detail the arguments made here, Chapter 2 provides a broad statistical exploration of the postwar ecology of states and its implications for civil war. Statistical analysis, rather than a study of particular cases, is best suited to surveying the broad macro-historical effects of the international system on the length of civil wars. Data on civil wars from 1816 to 1997 is analyzed to understand the effects of the international system, weak state structure, the Cold War, and intervention on the duration of civil wars. A technical appendix is included at the end of the book for readers interested in the details of coding and methodology.

Chapters 3 through 6 expand one aspect of the argument with illustrations from historical examples. Chapter 3 looks at the weaknesses of recently independent states and their impact on lengthy civil wars. I describe the international processes that led to the dismantling of the colonial empires and the creation of large numbers of weak states, as well as the ways in which state weakness affects the duration of wars.

Chapter 4 deals with the counterargument that lengthy civil wars are due to hatreds bred of ethnic conflict. I criticize the notion that "ethnic" or "identity-based" civil wars are different from other types of war. Instead, I argue that identity-based civil wars are merely one variant of weak-state civil war, and are based in the same general processes as other civil wars of this era.

Chapter 5 examines the effect that the Cold War has had on prolonging civil wars. Rather than taking the communist/Western aspect of civil wars as a given, I argue that international actors constructed and imposed Cold War dimensions on many civil wars. Once a civil war was defined as communist by the superpowers, Cold War frameworks provided material and cognitive resources that increased the duration of these wars.

Chapter 6 discusses the impact that interstate interventions have had on the lengthening of civil wars. One major source of intervention has been the Cold War conflict, which encouraged partisan intervention in Third World conflicts. Additionally, international interventions are commonly perpetrated by states other than the superpowers, for reasons ranging from support of weak-state sovereignty to carrying out interstate aggression to policing civil unrest in the intervening country. These interventions, which often take place on both sides of the civil war, have contributed to the substantial increase in the duration of civil wars after 1945.

In Chapter 7 I reflect on the importance of recognizing the role played by the international system in lengthening the civil wars in this period, and speculate on ways in which the international community might constrain civil wars in weak states in the future.

2

World Patterns in Civil War Duration

THE STATISTICAL ANALYSES in this chapter test the arguments I have advanced thus far—specifically, the impact of a changing international ecology of states on civil war activity over the last two centuries. I also examine more targeted hypotheses regarding weak states, ethnic conflict, the influences of the Cold War, and the consequences of interstate intervention. To foreshadow the outcomes briefly, the statistical findings do strongly support the general argument that the international system has played a critical role in lengthening the civil wars in the late twentieth century.

The claims developed earlier are very broad in scope, addressing a worldwide shift in civil war activity over the last century. Any given historical case (or handful of cases) provides an insufficient basis for drawing conclusions regarding global trends of this scope. While statistical models do not capture the historical and political complexity of individual civil wars, they are able to provide valuable information on such broad empirical trends. A statistical approach has the advantage of highlighting general trends without being overly swayed by a few exceptions. Subsequent chapters look to specific cases for greater detail and give a more fine-grained treatment of arguments.

This study requires clear conceptualization and measurement of civil wars that is not biased across region or time. The general public receives more news and scholarship about some regions of the world than others. For instance, the news coverage of the conflict in Northern Ireland has been far greater than that of the civil war in the Sudan. Thus it is a shock to realize that the casualty figures for the thirty years of "troubles" in Northern Ireland are approximately 3,000, while the casualties for the twenty-year old civil war in the Sudan run in the millions (Brogan 1998; Sivard 1996). Moreover, there is a political aspect to the labeling of a conflict as a civil war, rather than a "police action" or "control of foreign elements." Since the results of the analyses can only be as reliable as the data that went into them, care must be taken to ensure that the definition and measurement of civil wars is consistent and unbiased.

The data on civil wars that is used in this book comes from the Correlates of War dataset (Small and Singer 1982; updated in Sarkees 2000). The chief advantage of this dataset is that it uses explicit and objective criteria for defining wars, in contrast to other sources of civil war data that disproportionately emphasize certain regions or certain time periods (for instance, see Luard 1972; Richardson 1960; Clodfelter 1992). The Correlates of War define civil wars according to three criteria. First, the war must be between the state and a societal opposition group, rather than among societal groups. Secondly, both groups of combatants must actively participate in the civil war. This criterion distinguishes between a war and a massacre in which one group is slaughtered without significant resistance. Third, the yearly toll of casualties must be greater than a thousand battle deaths. This criterion limits the list to large-scale civil wars. The battle casualty criterion also provides dates on the start and end of civil wars, which is used to calculate the duration of the war. While a Correlates of War civil war may be preceded or followed by years of lower-intensity conflict, the battle death criterion includes only years of high-intensity conflict. By using these criteria I do not mean to imply that lower-intensity conflicts are unimportant or that they cannot have significant political or social consequences—as the examples of Northern Ireland and South Africa demonstrate. But the objective criteria of the Correlates of War dataset provide comparability across countries and historical periods that is critical to this study.

The criterion of 1,000 war-related casualties per year is not as arbitrary as it might seem at first. Most civil wars have well over a thousand casualties, and most events we would intuitively consider riots or assassinations are closer to fifty than a thousand. For instance, the average number of casualties per year for a war in the Correlates of War dataset is roughly 20,000—a figure based on casualties for the state, as data on insurgent casualties are often missing in the dataset. Thus it is a very conservative estimate of the number of deaths per year. Other datasets with different casualty thresholds—such as Regan (2000), who includes wars with a minimum of 200 casualties, or Fearon (2002), who includes wars with 1,000 casualties over the entire course of the war and a minimum yearly average of 100—result in lists of wars that are similar to the Correlates of War.

Using three different statistical "lenses," I explore aspects of civil war activity covered in my general argument. I begin with a very broad lens, which looks at trends over the past two centuries in the overall number of civil wars in the world. These statistical analyses seek to discern whether historical changes in the world polity are responsible for increases or decreases in the number of ongoing civil wars. Next, I focus on nations—both those that have experienced wars and those that have not—to determine which characteristics render a country vulnerable to civil war. In particular, I focus on hypotheses regarding the strength of the state. Finally, I focus the lens very closely, to examine each civil war fought from 1945 to 1997. Here, I seek to find out whether aspects of the war itself, such as the presence of third-party intervention, affect the rapidity with which wars are resolved. I hope to determine why many wars, once begun, are very difficult to end.

By looking at civil war with such different lenses I am able to test a wide range of arguments and hypotheses, thereby gaining a rich understanding of the factors responsible for the lengthy civil wars of the contemporary era. The result is the following summary findings of statistical analyses. For those interested in the details of the data and the statistical methods, technical information and complete statistical models are presented in the Appendix.

The World Polity and the Creation of War-Prone States

The first set of arguments addresses historical changes in the world polity and the consequences for the occurrence of civil war. I begin with statistical analyses that look for a statistical relationship between temporal trends in the international sphere and temporal trends in the number of civil wars that occur throughout the world.

Various postwar world polity processes were responsible for the creation, protection, and maintenance of the weak states that are prone to civil war. To begin with, international actors and norms encouraged decolonization, which led to the creation of many new and very weak states. The postwar climate of opinion fostered the decline of interstate wars and protected the territorial integrity of these states. In addition, the illegitimacy of secession in international law and norms prevented recently independent states from splintering into smaller, more manageable states. These processes fundamentally reshaped the ecology of states over the past century. I expect that these trends will be statistically correlated with increased civil war activity.

Of all the changes in the ecology of the international system, decolonization is perhaps the most dramatic. A large proportion of the states in the world today have been created out of former colonies. A handful of these amassed the economic and administrative resources to fight their way to independence. Most former colonies, however, did not develop the capabilities and resources that accompanied the rise of European states. These former colonial states have experienced the majority of civil wars since World War II.

Figure 2.1 displays these trends over time. The graph shows the number of ex-colonial states in existence over the past two centuries, as well as the number of ongoing civil wars. Both trends are measured as ten-year averages and smoothed to highlight the overall pattern. As one can see, the number of former colonial states grew modestly from 1800 to 1840, followed by a period of stability from roughly 1840 to 1950. Following World War II, the number of ex-colonial states explodes from around 30 to almost 120—an increase of nearly 400 percent. The trend finally levels off in the 1980s, by which time few colonies remained in existence. Figure 2.1 also shows the number of ongoing civil wars, which roughly mirrors the number of ex-colonial states. Civil war activity grows in the early- and mid-nineteenth century, following a first wave of decolonization, and increases dramatically following the wave of decolonization in the post-World War II era. While temporal correlation is insufficient to determine causation, the graph is suggestive of a relationship between ex-colonial states and civil war activity in the world.

The second major world polity process affecting the ecology of states

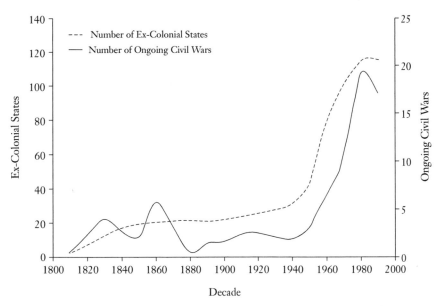

Figure 2.1 Correspondence of Former Colonial States and Ongoing Civil Wars, 1816–1997

is the decline of interstate war. Typical of the post-1945 period are strong international laws and norms against territorial war, and a dramatic decrease in the incidence of such wars. In an era when states no longer routinely go to war over territory, even very weak states may survive. This condition may set the stage for civil conflict. Although the laws of the international system have formally protected the territorial borders of weak states, these states nevertheless bear the consequences of their lack of military capability. Military weakness manifests itself through the inability to prevent or resolve civil wars. Figure 2.2 shows the number of ongoing interstate wars, as well as the number of civil wars, from 1816 to 1997. Again, lines represent smoothed decadal averages. Except for a lull in the early nineteenth century, interstate war has persisted at high levels over time. Despite fluctuations, interstate war has been endemic over the past two centuries. Yet a conspicuous decrease in interstate war can be seen starting in the late 1960s and continuing until the present (Hironaka 1998; Zacher 2001). This dropoff in interstate war coincides with the recent acceleration in civil war activity.

The reluctance of the international community to recognize or support secessionist regions has implications for civil war. While many re-

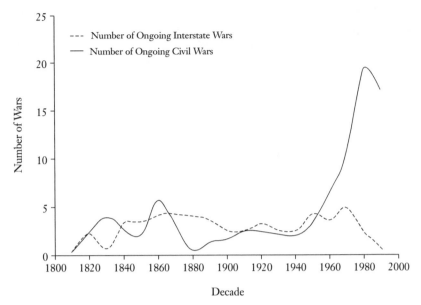

Figure 2.2 Correspondence of Interstate Wars and Ongoing Civil Wars, 1816–1997

gions have attempted to declare secession in the past century, the international community has had the final word on which are granted full sovereign status and which remain in limbo, such as Cyprus and Taiwan. Since secession has been relatively rare in the twentieth century, one can only speculate on the effect that an international norm allowing secession would have on civil wars. In a more favorable climate many of the large and unstable states might break up into more manageable sub-units. Huge territories with widely dispersed population centers like Nigeria or the Congo (formerly Zaire) are difficult to govern and seem particularly susceptible to civil strife. Secession or reorganization might result in more stable societies. Also, one might contrast the relatively peaceful breakup of the Soviet Union, in which the international system accepted the former Soviet republics as sovereign states, with the violent breakup of Yugoslavia in which Bosnia-Herzegovina and Croatia were not internationally recognized as states until their civil wars had been concluded. The general refusal of the world polity to countenance secession has prevented splintering as a possible solution, and thus indirectly encouraged civil wars.

Figure 2.3 is a graph showing the level of international antisecession discourse over the past two centuries, as well as the number of ongo-

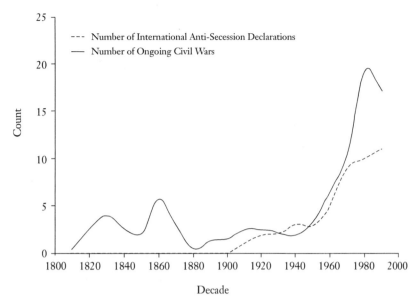

Figure 2.3 Correspondence of International Anti-Secessionist Declarations and Ongoing Civil Wars, 1816–1997

ing civil wars. The dashed line shows the cumulative number of international declarations made against secession. The figure shows that the number of anti-secessionist declarations grows slowly over the course of the twentieth century, but declarations against secession increase after 1945, as large numbers of ex-colonies achieve independence. In the 1990s, the number of new anti-secessionist declarations trails off, perhaps because the normative position against secession had been solidified in international law by that point. Conversely, this might reflect a shift toward greater acceptance of secession within the international community (see Chapter 7). In any case, the growth of anti-secessionist declarations corresponds with the number of ongoing civil wars in the world. Again, correlation does not directly imply causal processes, but is suggestive. Further analysis is needed to verify the relationship between anti-secession discourse and civil war.

Statistical Results

Here I examine whether decolonization, decline in territorial war, and discouragement of secession are statistically correlated with changes in civil war activity. These multivariate statistical models provide a firmer basis for drawing conclusions about causal relationships, compared to the visual correlations observed in Figures 2.1 to 2.3. The following statistical analysis examines the number of civil wars being fought anywhere in the world in each year from 1816 to 1997. The variable being explained (the "dependent variable") is a numeric count of the ongoing civil wars occurring in each year. This count is analyzed using a negative binomial regression model, which is appropriate for variables of this type. Table 2.1 summarizes the main findings of this statistical analysis. Complete statistical tables and more detailed information on the coding of the variables can be found in the Appendix.

The results of this analysis indicate that world polity processes and the changing ecology of states have contributed to the very large increase in civil war activity. As the number of colonial states and volume of anti-secession discourse increased, so too have the numbers of ongoing civil wars. And, as the number of interstate wars decreases, a corresponding increase is observed in civil war activity. All of these findings are statistically significant, meaning that there is confidence that the estimated effects are greater than zero.

The effect of each variable is most easily interpreted by its impact, in terms of percentage change, on the dependent variable. Values in Table 2.1 list the impact for each 1-point change in a variable. For in-

Table 2.1 Effects of decolonization, interstate war, and anti-secessionism on the number of ongoing civil wars, 1816–1997

Variables	Effect on the number of ongoing civil wars (per 1-point change in variable) Model 1	Total estimated impact on number of civil wars from 1945–1997
Ex-colonial states (as percent of all states)	+5%***	+165%
Recent interstate war (number in past 5 years)	−2%***	+30%
International anti-secession declarations	+10%***	+114%

***$p<.01$, **$p<.05$, *$p<.10$, two-tailed test.

stance, a 1-point change in the ex-colonial states variable (measured as the percentage of all states that are ex-colonies) is statistically associated with a 5 percent change in the number of ongoing civil wars. These results indicate that the worldwide increase in ex-colonial states has had a substantial effect on the number of ongoing civil wars in the world. Table 2.1 also shows the percentage change in the number of ongoing civil wars that is estimated to result from observed shifts in the independent variables between 1945 and 1997. The proliferation of ex-colonial states in the world from 1945 to 1997 contributed to an estimated 165 percent increase in the number of civil wars. In other words, civil wars increased by over one and one-half times in the latter part of the twentieth century as a consequence of the growing number of ex-colonial states in the world.

The effect of interstate war has also had an effect on ongoing civil wars. Table 2.1 shows that as the number of interstate wars decreases, the number of civil wars increases (and vice versa). Every additional year of interstate war is associated with a 2 percent reduction in civil war activity. Likewise, each decline in interstate war is associated with a 2 percent increase in civil war activity. Because interstate wars declined substantially from 1945 to 1997, the corresponding effect on civil wars is positive, cumulating to an overall 30 percent increase in the number of ongoing civil wars.

Anti-secessionist discourse in the international system is also associated with growth in the number of civil wars in the world. For every major international declaration against the legitimacy of secession made by an international organization, the number of civil wars increases by an average of 10 percent, as shown in Table 2.1. From 1945 to 1997, the growing international consensus against secession contributed to a 114 percent increase in the number of civil wars, controlling for other factors.

Taken together, these results suggest that world polity processes have strongly influenced the number of civil wars in the world. While civil wars have always been a feature of the international system, their explosion since 1945 has been due in large part to these changing dynamics of the international system. The reader should keep in mind these international processes as we turn our attention to the factors that make some states more prone to civil wars than others within this international climate.

The Effects of Weak States

How do macro-level trends regarding decolonization, interstate war, and secession generate more civil war? These historical changes led to a new ecology of states, in which a large number of weak states came into existence and survived. The argument contends that these weak states are much more likely to experience lengthy civil wars than are stronger, more established states. The statistical analyses that follow explore the relationship between state strength and the occurrence of civil war.

Weak states are vulnerable to lengthy wars because they lack the resources and organizational capacity to terminate the domestic conflicts that arise. Frequently, weak states are incapable of controlling their own territory, creating opportunities for insurgent groups to strengthen in remote areas before challenging the state in more central locations. Indeed, many insurgent groups do not venture into government-held areas, but are nearly impossible to root out of their peripheral strongholds. Additionally, both insurgent groups and the state are often aided by other countries, which provide the resources to prolong conflicts in these weak states. Weak states are typically unable to control their borders and thus to limit the flow of resources to the insurgent groups.

I explore two main dimensions of state strength: *material resources* and *institutional structure*. First, and most obviously, states may be weak because they lack the basic material resources to function and maintain order. This is reflected in a nation's basic level of economic and military resources. Second, weak states may lack sufficient bureaucratic and institutional structures to ensure the functioning of government. For instance, many newly independent states lacked trained civil servants and bureaucracy—and even domestic communications and transportation. Such countries could barely operate school systems, courts, welfare systems, or other essentials for societal functioning, not to mention the kinds of complex (and trustworthy) bureaucracies needed to engage in negotiations with conflicting parties or insurgent groups. Institutional structure is reflected by the expansion of state bureaucracy and services.

Institutional structure is also indirectly reflected by the historical period in which states achieved independence. States that became independent after 1945 were created during a period in which interstate wars, and even wars of independence, were rare. These states tended to have insufficient bureaucratic infrastructures and government institutions, particularly when colonial powers hastily departed. Thus the historical period in which a state became independent may serve as a proxy for the capabilities of state bureaucracy and institutions.

The statistical analyses below focus on *states* and the particular characteristics that make some states more or less prone to civil war when compared to others. This is in contrast with the previous analysis, which looked at global trends in civil war activity over *time* but did not identify which states were experiencing civil wars. I employ a statistical technique known as "event history analysis" (Tuma and Hannan 1984). This statistical approach takes as given that each state is potentially at risk of experiencing a civil war in every year. The analysis focuses on the rate of occurrence ("hazard rate") of civil war activity for states. Here I define "activity" as a year in which a civil war is occurring. Thus I am analyzing the *rate of war-years*, not the simple number of wars a country experiences. Consequently, the analysis incorporates and reflects the intuitive notion that long wars represent more "civil war activity" than short ones. In this framework it is possible to determine which characteristics of states are associated with higher (or lower) rates of occurrence of civil war activity.

Table 2.2 shows the effects of resources and institutional structure on the rate at which states experience civil war activity over the period from 1945 to 1997. Analyses covering a broader historical span are discussed later. The results of Table 2.2 suggest that weak states—

Table 2.2 Effects of state strength on civil war years, 1945–1997[a]

Variables	Effect on incidence of civil war years (per 1-point change in variable)
	Model 2
Economic and military capability	−36%***
Governmental capacity	−48%***
Post–1945 independence	+26%*

***$p < .01$, **$p < .05$, *$p < .10$, two-tailed test.

a. Country population, territorial area, and democracy were included as control variables but are not presented in this table.

measured in economic/military capability, indicators of institutional structure, and post-1945 independence—are much more likely to experience years of civil war than states that are strong on those dimensions.

For example, a 1-unit increase in a state's economic and military capabilities results in a 36 percent decrease in its likelihood of having a civil war year. The negative sign indicates that the greater the economic and military capability of the country, the lower its rate of experiencing civil war in a given year. Economic/military capability is measured by an index that includes, among other things, GDP per capita and military expenditures. For instance, the United States, one of the high scorers on this index, averaged 2.73 in this period, while Laos scored below the mean with an average of −0.24. Using the percentage change estimates in Table 2.2, countries with economic/military capacity similar to the United States have a 73 percent lower rate of civil war years compared to countries similar to Laos, controlling for other factors. Of course, when additional factors are taken into account, the disparity in war activity is greater still.

Two measures of institutional structure are also tested for their effects on the probability of civil wars. The first measure is the governmental capacity of the state. This measure reflects the level of functional services provided by the state and is an index composed of an indicator of the effectiveness of the legislature, primary and secondary school enrollments per capita, and amount of railroad track per square mile. These are intended as a general measure of government services and capacity (rather than indicators of the proximate causes of civil war). The negative sign implies that the more governmental capacity a state has, the lower the incidence of civil war years. The United States, for example, averaged 1.97 in this period, compared to Laos with a score of −1.38. A difference of this magnitude is associated with a dramatic 89 percent reduction in the rate of civil war activity, controlling for other factors.

A third measure of institutional structure emphasizes the period in which a state became independent. As discussed earlier, states such as the United States, which became independent before 1945, were forced to develop more institutional structure than states that have become independent more recently. Not only have older states had more time to develop bureaucratic structures, but also they typically faced greater international pressures to develop military capabilities when compared to younger states. States such as Laos, which became independent after 1945, have a 26 percent greater rate of civil war years than older states. This effect of the period of independence is net of other factors, like state weakness, that combine to produce a very high rate of civil war years among countries like Laos.

In the period from 1945 to 1997, weak states were far more likely to experience civil war than states that were strong on these dimensions. Looking back to earlier eras, has weakness always led to civil war, or is the post-1945 international ecology of states distinctive? I argue the latter conclusion: the contemporary ecology supports and maintains states that are exceedingly weak relative to others. In every period, of course, some states are weaker than other states. Before 1945, however, the disparities were not so great and thus relative weakness did not mean substantially more civil wars. Prior to World War II, the disparity in strength between the state and the opposition was great enough that civil wars ended quickly and decisively and recurrences of civil war were prevented. Consequently, weak states of that era did not have drastically prolonged civil wars, as they do after 1945.

This historical change is evident in the results presented in Table 2.3. This table shows the effect of the same independent variables upon the rate of civil war years in different historical periods. Economic and military capability, which is a significant negative predictor of civil war years in the 1945–1997 period, is not statistically significant in either the nineteenth century (1816–1899) or the early twentieth century (1900–1944). This is shown by the nonsignificant findings in the left and middle columns of Table 2.3. Instead, it is only after 1945 that economic and military capability significantly affect the rate of civil war years experienced by a given nation.

One factor, however—governmental capacity, a measure of institutional structure—is a negative and significant predictor of civil war years for all three periods, from 1816 to 1997. Governmental capacity is measured by the effectiveness of the legislature and the amount of railroad track per square mile. (Primary and secondary school enrollments per capita were not included because data is not available for the nineteenth century.) In all three historical periods, effective government bureaucratic and political systems reduce the rate of civil war activity, controlling for other factors. The third measure of state weak-

Table 2.3   Effects of state strength in different historical periods on civil war years, 1816–1997[a]

Variables	Effect on incidence of civil war years (per 1-point change in variable)		
	Model 3 1816–1899	Model 4 1900–1944	Model 5 1945–1997
Economic and military capability	Not significant[b]	Not significant[b]	−36%***
Governmental capacity	−63%***	−60%***	−48%***
Post–1945 independence	—	—	+26%*

***$p<.01$, **$p<.05$, *$p<.10$, two-tailed test

a. Country population, territorial area, and democracy were included as control variables but are not presented in this table.

b. By convention, the effects of variables that are not statistically significant are assumed to be not reliably different from zero.

ness, post-1945 independence, could not be included in the historical models, since these states did not exist in the earlier time periods.

In sum, state economic and military weakness has not always led to lengthy civil wars. Instead, the weak states of the late twentieth century are distinctive in their vulnerability, compared to weak states in earlier historical periods. This is presumably because changes in the world polity have resulted in the creation of states that are far weaker, in a relative sense, compared to their peers. In addition, international flows of resources and aid to insurgents have exacerbated the vulnerability of weak states in this period.

Ethnic Conflict

Here I briefly address one common explanation for civil war: ethnic rivalry and conflict (see Chapter 4 for an extended discussion). Scholarship on ethnic conflict has suggested that the ties binding ethnic groups are stronger than the political ties that have traditionally bound together the opposing parties in civil wars (Saideman 2001; Vanhanen 1999; Kaufmann 1996). These arguments suggest that the nature and goals of ethnic civil wars differ from those of traditional civil wars fought over political ends—and are much more intractable. The strength of ethnic ties is commonly invoked to explain the long duration of civil wars in recent decades. Potent ethnic ties, it is argued, lead ethnic groups to carry on a fight when other groups would surrender, despite hardship, casualties, and war weariness.

I contend that structural factors, rather than group identities, are primarily responsible for the level of civil war activity a country experiences. The dynamics and length of contemporary civil wars are due to the weakness of the state, rather than to the ethnic ties of the group prosecuting the war. Ethnic groups are oftentimes participants in such wars, but the causal factors generating intractable wars tend to be structural. In brief, it is the structure of the state—specifically, its lack of material resources and institutional structures—that encourages the formation of ethnic and other identity-based opposition groups. As a result, political parties in recently independent states are often based upon nonideological social identities such as ethnicity or geographic region. Thus the emphasis on the "ethnic" aspect of civil wars is spurious; the real effect is due to the structural weaknesses of the state.

Here I present statistical analyses that address this issue: do nations with many ethnic and/or linguistic groups experience more civil war activity than those that are more ethnically homogeneous? In the following analysis, ethnic diversity is included in an event-history model of civil war years. If ethnic groups are a common basis for lengthy wars, then ethnically homogeneous nations should experience civil war years at a lower rate. Ethnic diversity is measured, as is standard in this literature, on the basis of on an index from 1 to 100 that represents the heterogeneity of ethnic and linguistic groups in a country (Taylor and Hudson 1973). For instance, the United States scores 49 on this measure, while ethnically homogeneous Japan scores 1 and Yugoslavia scores 73. This follows in the footsteps of Sambanis (2001), who found that this measure of ethnic diversity was a significant predictor of ethnic civil war.

The analyses presented in Table 2.4 show that indicators of state weakness are better predictors of civil war years than ethnic diversity, casting doubt on ethnic explanations of civil war. In the first column (Model 6), before other factors are taken into account, we see that ethnic diversity by itself is a strong predictor of civil war years. For instance, according to the percentage-change figures given in Model 6, an ethnically diverse country like Yugoslavia would have a 27 percent greater rate of experiencing civil war years than a country like the United States, and a 205 percent greater rate compared to an ethnically homogeneous country like Japan.

However, when the weak state indicators are taken into account in Model 7, the ethnic diversity effect ceases to be statistically significant.

Table 2.4 Effects of ethnic diversity on civil war years, 1945–1997[a]

Variables	Effect on incidence of civil war years (per 1-point change in variable)	
	Model 6	Model 7
Economic and military capability	—	−23%**
Governmental capacity	—	−48%***
Post–1945 independence	—	+28%**
Ethno-linguistic diversity	1%***	Not significant[b]

***p<.01, **p<.05, *p<.10, two-tailed test

a. Country population, territorial area, and democracy were included as control variables but are not presented in this table.

b. By convention, the effects of variables that are not statistically significant are assumed to be not reliably different from zero.

This loss of statistical significance indicates that the effect of ethnic diversity is not reliably different from zero and suggests that the apparent effect of ethnic diversity was, in fact, spurious. Rather, the weak state variables remain statistically significant, proving to be better statistical correlates of civil war. The greater incidence of war in states like Yugoslavia compared to the states like the United States and Japan can instead be attributed to differences in state strength. This provides evidence in favor of the weak state argument over ethnic conflict arguments.

I NOW TURN to a close examination of civil wars themselves, to determine why some take much longer to resolve than others. Rather than examine the world- and nation-level factors that encourage civil war, these analyses focus on aspects of the wars that increase or reduce their duration. In other words, given that a war breaks out, what factors make wars last longer? The analysis focuses on the set of civil wars that have been fought since 1945. The dependent variable is the number of days that the civil war lasted. Event-history duration models are used to estimate the effects that being identified as a Cold War conflict had on the length of civil wars.

The Cold War

One set of models examines the effects of the Cold War and related military interventions on the length of civil wars. The Cold War, which

lasted from 1945 to 1989, provided a global framework of material resources and potent ideologies that perpetuated local civil wars. In some
sense, domestic civil wars were local instantiations of the world-level
ideological conflict and could not be resolved until the Cold War itself
ended. When the Cold War finally ceased, lengthy communist civil
wars such as those in Guatemala, El Salvador, Nicaragua, and Peru
ended as well.

The sites of Cold War conflicts were typically the weak states of the
Third World, rather than the politically and economically developed
countries that were explicitly connected to the Warsaw Pact or the
North Atlantic Treaty Organization. In many cases, the local political
actors involved in the civil wars of these weak states often did not initially perceive the conflict as relating to communism or pro-Western
ideologies. Instead, external actors such as the superpowers often imposed Cold War frameworks and interpretations upon Third World
conflicts, an argument that is developed in Chapter 5. In any case, civil
wars that became polarized along Cold War camps often gained international attention and, in many cases, superpower intervention.

Table 2.5 shows the effects of the Cold War on the duration of civil
wars. The results of Model 8 show that civil wars involving pro- or
anti-communist forces lasted 141 percent longer, on average, than civil
wars that were not classified as Cold War conflicts (or, equivalently, the
rate at which such wars are resolved is 59 percent lower. For details, see
the Appendix). In addition, after the Berlin Wall fell in 1989, the expected duration of communist civil wars dropped by 91 percent as
shown by the post-Cold War variable (reflecting a more than ten-fold
increase in the rate of resolution).

Table 2.5 Effects of the Cold War on duration of civil wars, 1945–1997[a]

	Effect on duration of civil wars	
Variables	Model 8	Model 9
Cold War civil war	+141%***	+72%**
Post–Cold War years	−91%***	−92%***
Superpower intervention	—	+141%***

***p<.01, **p<.05, *p<.10, two-tailed test
a. Country population, democracy, historical year, and battle deaths/year were included as
control variables but are not shown in this table.

Part of the increased duration of Cold War civil wars was due to superpower intervention in these wars. As Model 9 shows, civil wars with superpower intervention lasted 141 percent longer than wars without superpower intervention on average. However, Cold War civil wars were not merely longer because of superpower intervention. The effect of the Cold War civil war variable in the table remains positive and significant, resulting in an average increase of 72 percent in the length of conflicts, even after taking into account the effect of superpower intervention. In combination, Cold War ideologies and superpower intervention resulted in wars that typically lasted over three times longer than other wars.

Interstate Intervention

Another major influence on the length of civil wars among weak states has been the tremendous amount of interstate intervention evident in the post-World War II civil wars. Interstate intervention is not new to this historical period, of course; states have intervened in the domestic affairs of each other since the international system has existed (Hoffman 1984). But the large population of weak states created after 1945 has encouraged more intervention in civil wars than in previous historical periods. In addition, the nature of intervention has changed since 1945. Historically, intervention tended to occur on behalf of only one side of a civil war. During the early nineteenth century, the Great Powers of Europe conferred and often acted jointly to squelch a civil war. In the interventions of the post-World War II world, however, it has been common for both the state and the opposition group to benefit from international support and intervention, creating a civil war fueled by extra-national resources.

Furthermore, many more states intervened in the affairs of their fellow states in the contemporary period than in the past. Historically, the Great Powers of Europe would intervene in conflicts of interest to them, as would a regional power such as the United States in its "backyard" of Central America. Less militarily powerful states would rarely intervene in foreign civil wars. By the late twentieth century, however, this had changed. In addition to the superpowers, former colonial powers, regional powers, and neighboring states increasingly began to join in the civil wars of other states.

Table 2.6 shows the effects of intervention on the length of civil wars. This analysis, like the previous one, examines the duration of civil wars. The results presented in Model 10 suggest that civil wars with interstate intervention are dramatically longer than civil wars in which intervention did not occur. On average, civil wars with interstate intervention, broadly defined, are 300 percent longer than wars without intervention. This effect is extremely large, suggesting that intervention is one of the biggest factors in lengthening contemporary civil wars. The results of Model 11 separate out the impact of intervention, generally, from those cases that experience intervention on behalf of *both sides* of a civil war. In this model, the presence of any third-party intervener increases war duration by 156 percent, and the presence of two-sided intervention lengthens wars by an additional 92 percent.

In addition, the results presented in Model 12 suggest that the effects of interstate intervention are not simply due to the superpowers. On the one hand, it is the case that civil wars that involve superpower intervention tend to last 72 percent longer than civil wars without it. Conflicts in states such as Angola, for instance, which receive intervention on both sides and by the superpowers (actually, in the case of Angola, superpowers intervened on both sides) will be 538 percent longer on average than a civil war without any intervention. On the other hand, the effects of any intervention, and of two-sided intervention, are still significant when the superpower variable is included in the model, indicating that superpower intervention is not the entire story. Interventions by former colonial powers, regional powers, and neighboring states also play a substantial role in lengthening civil wars.

Table 2.6   Effects of interstate intervention on duration of civil wars, 1945–1997[a]

	Effect on duration of civil wars		
Variables	Model 10	Model 11	Model 12
Intervention	+300%***	+156%***	+92%**
Intervention on both sides	—	+92%**	+92%**
Superpower intervention	—	—	+72%**

***$p<.01$, **$p<.05$, *$p<.10$, two-tailed test.

a. Country population, democracy, historical year, and battle deaths/year were included as control variables but are not shown in this table.

Conclusion

Statistical results strongly support the arguments developed in Chapter 1. The world polity set the stage for a greater number of civil wars in the post-1945 era. Changes that resulted in decolonization, the decline of interstate warfare, and international norms against secession produced a world in which weak states proliferated and civil wars were more common. A closer examination of nation-states shows that weak states are the ones that experience the majority of those new civil wars. Finally, interstate intervention and Cold War alignments further lengthen those conflicts that do break out.

The strength of statistical models is their ability to show the broad historical trends that cannot be discerned from the examination of one or even a handful of individual cases. Scholars who study individual civil wars may speculate that the international climate or the origins of the state provided the circumstances that encouraged a particular lengthy civil war, but without broad comparison to other cases, particularly to cases of states with similar structures that did not experience civil war, it is difficult to provide supporting empirical evidence. At the same time, the use of statistical models does not invalidate the need for close historical studies of particular states and civil wars; rather, it can supplement these case studies by placing them in a broad historical and international context.

3

Weak States and the Difficulties of State-building

THE FUNDAMENTAL DISORGANIZATION of many recently independent states is the key to understanding contemporary civil conflict. The course of civil wars has always depended upon the nature of the states that gave rise to the conflict. As Charles Tilly has claimed for civil wars in Europe: "The possibility and character of revolution changed with the organization of states and systems of states; they will change again with future alterations of state power. Revolutions are no longer what they were because states are no longer what they were" (Tilly 1993:5). As the post-World War II world became populated with a new kind of state that was weaker and more ineffectual, civil wars became increasingly intractable.

The distinction between the weaker states of the Third World and the stronger, more established European states is ground well trodden by scholars (Migdal 2001, 1988; Herbst 2000; Holsti 1996). Studies have examined the disparate capabilities of weak and strong states as based upon the historical conditions of the international system present at their founding (Herbst 2000; Tilly 1992; Jackson and Rosberg 1982; Poggi 1978; Nettl 1968; Bendix 1964). The implications for civil war have not been seriously considered, but it is the insights of this literature on state-building that provide the basis for explaining why weak states are vulnerable to protracted civil wars.

The discussion of the challenges of state-building begins with a brief

53

review of state-building in the West, to provide an illustrative contrast to the experiences of recently independent states. I then look at the hurdles faced by newly independent states, and the role of the international system in bolstering their *de jure* (if not *de facto*) sovereignty. Somalia serves as an example of a recently independent weak state in which the failure of state-building resulted in a lengthy civil war. Finally, I enumerate and discuss aspects of "state weakness" that most directly contribute to protracted civil wars.

State-building in the West and the Third World

On paper, most states look surprisingly similar. All contemporary states claim a centralized government, a bounded territory, and a population with formal citizenship rights—the central elements that define statehood. They also maintain various trappings of statehood, including a flag, a national anthem, a seat in the United Nations, public education, economic policy, and environmental legislation, to name only a few (McNeely 1995). Neo-institutional theorists argue that these similarities among states are not coincidental, nor do they necessarily represent efficient adaptation to local needs. Rather, this isomorphism reflects an international model of the idealized state—in effect, a set of blueprints for legitimate formal structures and policies (McNeely 1995; Meyer et al. 1997). New governments typically look to other states or to the international community as a whole for examples of how to organize and govern. The world polity, in turn, is filled with policy professionals, development banks, and international organizations that encourage and provide resources to facilitate the adoption of standardized state structures and policies, based on abstract models that could be applied anywhere. Jepperson (2001:13) writes: "It appear[s] that [state policies were] being constructed more for an *imagined* society than for real societies . . . people in modern societies are constantly developing, redeveloping, and enacting *models* of society: modern social worlds are highly theorized, hence 'imagined'" (italics in the original).

Weak states seek to conform to the "imagined" state for several reasons, not the least of which is that such models are cognitively dominant in the world, making it difficult to imagine alternate forms. Conformity to the "imagined" state also provides an important source of legitimacy for fragile states, and is a requisite for international recognition and aid. Contemporary weak states thus have a strong incentive to give the appearance of conforming to the idealized model of the state by adopting formal state structures that resemble those of the established states of the industrialized West (Meyer et al. 1997). In contrast, states that fail to sufficiently attend to the "imagined" attributes of statehood required by the international system risk being deemed nonstates by the international community—potentially resulting in the withdrawal of international development aid, or even invasion. Taiwan, for instance, has not been able to meet the international requirements of statehood for political reasons, thus does not qualify for some forms of international aid. Additionally, Taiwan does not merit the same degree of international protection in case of territorial invasion by the People's Republic of China that recognized nation-states such as (South) Korea or Vietnam might obtain.

In Western states there is typically a close correspondence between the actual realities of state practice and the policies and structures of the "imagined" state. Strong governments deliver substantial services such as the protection of citizens, the enforcement of legislation, and the relatively fair dispensation of justice. Yet even strong states experience occasional decoupling between policy and practice. Not all government bureaucracies are as efficient as they claim to be, and at times those inefficiencies hide deeper sins of mismanagement or corruption. In comparison with many recently independent weak states, however, governments of strong states live up to their promises relatively well. As political scientist Joel Migdal describes: "[T]oday, for those of us in the West, the state has been part of our natural landscape. Its presence, its authority, its place behind so many rules that fashion the minutiae of our lives, have all been so pervasive that it is difficult for us to imagine the situation being otherwise. We accept the rightness of a state's having high capabilities to extract, penetrate, regulate, and appropriate—in short, a strong state" (Migdal 1988:15).

In contrast, weak states often adopt the trappings of the imagined state without having the underlying capacities to carry out the promises implied by such structures and policies. In these cases, the functional aspects of the state may substantially depart from the implied promises of the imagined state. Essential governmental services are unavailable or corrupted. Rationalized bureaucratic systems in which office-holders act as agents of the state are also lacking. Instead, office-holders may act as agents of local networks, kinship groups, or in their own self-interest. Weak state governments may be unable to protect their own citizens from roaming bandits, guerrillas, or even from the state-run army and police forces. These weaknesses provide the preconditions for lengthy civil war.

Conformity to the imagined state engenders support from the international community that bolsters the sovereignty of weak states, even in the absence of functional infrastructure. For a better understanding of the disjunction between the functional and the imagined, I review the history of state-building in the West to provide a baseline to which newly independent states can be compared. The states formed since 1945 face challenges similar to those met by the European states in centuries past, but the conditions of independence have posed some additional challenges. The contemporary international community has played a crucial role in maintaining weak, or even defunct, states.

One cautionary note: the distinction between "strong" and "weak" is not simply shorthand for "the West versus the rest." While the literature emphasizes the different historical origins of Western states compared to the Third World, this distinction does not map exactly onto the distinction between strong states and weak states. Some states traditionally categorized as Third World states—especially Latin American states such as Argentina and Brazil and states in the Middle East such as Israel and Egypt—more closely fit the profile of strong states in terms of effective government structures and resources. In short, the distinction between strong and weak states should not be taken as a fixed distinction between Western versus non-Western status (see Japan, for example), but as a changing characteristic of states based upon their varying empirical characteristics.

State-building in the West

Because Western states function quite well today, it is easy to forget the tremendous efforts in previous centuries required to develop such capacities. Thus there is a corresponding tendency to underestimate the magnitude of the tasks faced by recently independent states, which for the most part have had to create governments from the ground up. Upon reflection, it is not at all surprising that recently independent states have been unable to overcome these hurdles in only a few decades. Indeed, one may even marvel that many have managed to avoid state collapse and prolonged civil war. This reminder of the labors of state construction in the West focuses particularly on the creation of rationalized bureaucratic structures, the development of taxation to provide internal resources for governmental maintenance, and the difficulties of territorial integration.

The challenges of state-building occupied the Western states for centuries, despite the advantages of resources, relatively high levels of internal order, and preexisting governmental structures evident in many Western countries. Stephen Skowronek observed that the United States did not fully rationalize its bureaucratic structure until the end of the nineteenth century. And, he argues, it was not until the early twentieth century that the United States succeeded in creating national institutions "free from the clutches of party domination, direct court supervision, and localistic orientations" (Skowronek 1982:15). The creation of a bureaucracy, judicial system, and other institutions of an effective government structure represented a tremendous achievement for the Western states.

The development of autonomous, rationalized bureaucratic structures was one of the most significant accomplishments of Western state-building. Max Weber, one of the fathers of sociology, developed the thesis that modern bureaucracies in the West tend to be run along rational-legal principles, in which bureaucratic actions are based upon objective rules rather than the whims of office-holders or reliance on tradition (Weber 1968). Officials thus represent the state, rather than local or kin interests. For Western states the development of rationalized bureaucracy was not the result of a natural evolution in Western states, but the result of centuries of effort. Reinhard Bendix has shown that the rationalization of the state bureaucracy in which civil servants were separated from "kinship loyalties, hereditary privileges, and property interests" was a major task for the European states that occupied them during much of the seventeenth and eighteenth centuries (Bendix 1964:106–7). Gianfranco Poggi has similarly argued that the arduous effort of "depersonalization" of state business, where "in their political relations individuals obey not one another but the law," took centuries to accomplish in Western states (Poggi 1978: 101–2).

The development of institutions for the reliable extraction of resources was a similarly laborious process in Europe. Procurement of resources was obviously a prerequisite for the development of substantial governmental and military capabilities, and yet those capabilities were in turn required to maintain an effective system of taxation. As Gabriel Ardant writes: "We cannot understand the history of the state if we are not convinced of the idea that taxation is a very difficult operation, even under a good administration, and that this difficulty has always weighed heavily upon the state" (Ardant 1975:165). Tax procedures that were fair, systematic, and relatively free of corruption took centuries to develop. The bureaucratization of taxation was greatly facilitated by the development of civil society in which taxes could be collected with only minimally coercive threats (Tilly 1992). And the development of an industrial economy, clearly a prerequisite to large-scale and effective taxation, also developed over the course of centuries. As Jeffrey Herbst (2000:113) concludes: "there is no better measure of a state's reach than its ability to collect taxes."

The European states also experienced major upheavals in their attempts to create a cohesive national identity among their peoples (Hobsbawm 1990). Prior to the nineteenth century, states rarely pursued national integration. Territories might be desired for strategic or economic reasons or, more likely, for the increased prestige they gave to the dynasty (Calhoun 1995). The people who lived on those territories were of little consequence, however, and tended to have no strong loyalties to one king or another. It was only in the nineteenth century that the idea of nationalism began to spread throughout Europe. States increasingly became coherent political units, economically self-sufficient and identifying themselves as single nations (Hobsbawm 1990; Gellner 1983). This integration did not happen overnight; the construction of a sense of unifying national identity took several decades in most states. Consider that even France of the early twentieth century, regarded as a very nationalist state, had not fully incorporated outlying regions. As late as World War I, some French soldiers conscripted from rural areas did not know the state for which they were fighting (Weber 1976).

One need not look to the distant past for examples of the difficulties of creating a rationalized, effective, and uncorrupted state structure in the West. Consider the difficulties in the adoption of the "rule of law" in Eastern Europe and the countries of the former Soviet Union during the 1990s. These countries had the benefit of existing institutions and substantial experience in lawmaking and government. Yet the sudden transition to capitalism and democracy entailed the creation of new laws managing economic and political behaviors, and subsequent shifts in governmental structure and citizen activity. The development of new institutions and rules was a significant challenge, and has not always proved successful.

The former communist states initially faced an onslaught of advisers from the international community who were primarily concerned with helping these states enact the right laws, naively assuming that institutions would naturally arise once the correct laws were in place (Sharlet 1997). The experts soon discovered, however, that having the right laws on the books was not enough (Carothers 1998; Murphey 1999). Instead, corruption and crime have flourished as governments struggled to build new institutions according to Western models. The post-Soviet states have illustrated the enormity of the task of switching a governmental structure from one form to another. The task of newly independent states has been even more challenging, as they often faced the creation of an entire government from scratch.

It is all too easy to take for granted the existence of a useful military, a functioning bureaucracy, and effective governance structures of modern states, forgetting that European states needed centuries to make the transition from a traditional to a rationalized state form. It is important to acknowledge that the failings of recently independent states are not due to an essential inferiority of character or excessive fallibility of leadership, but to the difficulties of state-building faced by all states.

The Legacy of Colonization

The states that achieved independence following World War II faced similar challenges to those experienced by the European states a century or two ago, with additional difficulties thrown in. Most colonies of the post-World War II era were unprepared for independence when it arrived. The imperial powers had put little thought or effort into building up domestic governance structures in their colonies, in large part because they did not foresee the rapid postwar decolonization of the world. A few colonies, such as India and Sri Lanka, had been allowed a degree of self-government, but other British colonies, such as British

Somaliland, were little more than trade outposts (Fieldhouse 1966; Laitin and Samatar 1987). French colonies, for instance, were typically ruled from Paris and had only minimal local political power, while the Belgian colonies were allowed no self-government at all until their abrupt independence in 1960 (Grimal 1965). Although colonies demanded immediate independence, in many cases they realistically did not possess the infrastructure for effective self-government (Somerville 1990). In short, they were unprepared for the immense challenges involved in the building of a working state.

Much like Western states of prior centuries, recently independent states of the Third World typically lacked effective bureaucratic and judicial structures. Bureaucracies were neither rationalized nor autonomous, but rather were heavily interpenetrated by "localistic orientations," also—less flatteringly—termed corruption, graft, or nepotism. In the words of one scholar, what was lacking was a bureaucracy that is "autonomous enough from society . . . that it is possible for it to make decisions that respond, not to specific interests in society, but to the aggregated requirements of an efficient management of economic, social, and cultural preferences" (Layachi 1995:186–7). Without an autonomous bureaucracy, citizens cannot be protected from local interests or, in many cases, from the malignant power of the state itself.

Often this lack of autonomy has made the state a puppet of societal influences, or alternatively, has allowed society to become the pawn of the self-interest of state leaders. Badie and Birnbaum (1983) have argued that government leaders are dependent upon the bureaucracy in many Third World countries because they lack an independent basis for power, a situation reminiscent of the courts of eighteenth-century Europe. Conversely, state leaders may distort the structure of the army or bureaucracy by stacking them with family or members of their own ethnic group in order to head off coup attempts and mutinies. For instance, President Ferdinand Marcos of the Philippines installed his wife, Imelda, as Minister of the Environment. As one might imagine, this tactic greatly impeded the effectiveness of environmental legislation in the Philippines, as government bureaucrats were reluctant to disclose environmental information to someone in no position to be impartial (Abracosa 1987). In sum, lack of autonomy of the state from societal influences, and vice versa, represents a major impediment to the effective functioning of government.

Newly independent states faced another major obstacle to the creation of an effective governmental apparatus: the lack of adequate material resources. The training of civil service personnel, the creation of bureaucratic mechanisms, and the daily maintenance of the state are all enhanced by abundant economic resources, whether in the West or the recently independent states. Frequently, however, these resources are lacking in the Third World, due to low levels of economic development and inefficient taxation systems. Economic self-sufficiency was not taken into consideration when colonies were granted independence, resulting in the creation of a population of impoverished states. The international system has stepped in, to some extent, with the provision of development aid. In most cases, though, international aid was no substitute for a functioning domestic economy. Starting out with a healthy economy did not, by itself, ensure a future of peace and stability among newly independent states, as Uganda and Zimbabwe illustrate. But a severe shortage of resources certainly did not help matters.

Colonial historians provide some insight into the poverty of recently independent states. There is debate in the literature as to whether the colonies suddenly became less economically profitable after 1945, creating an incentive for the imperial powers to grant their independence (Darwin 1991), or whether colonies had never been profitable in the first place (Fieldhouse 1966; Davis and Huttenbeck 1986). In either case, scholars agree that the majority of colonies were economically unprofitable at independence, with the exception of a very few cases such as India and perhaps Uganda, Malaysia, and Angola (Fieldhouse 1966). Unprofitable colonies that lacked natural resources and developed trade infrastructures quickly translated into impoverished states without the resources to provide for functional governmental structures.

Finally, colonial powers did not attend to the crucial issue of territorial integration. Often imperial powers controlled only the colonial capital or trading posts along the coast, and made no attempt to unify the territory into a single polity (Fieldhouse 1966). Again, this was largely because imperial powers were not expecting their colonies' independence and did not prepare for it. Thus they did not foresee that a common sense of national identity would be an asset in future decades (Fieldhouse 1966; Grimal 1965). Colonial fragmentation might even have been seen as advantageous to the imperial power, assuring it that indigenous peoples were unlikely to unite to throw off imperial domination. Moreover, the imperial powers probably did not have the resources or personnel to unify their colonies even had they agreed that was a desirable goal. In many colonies, only a handful of Europeans carried out administrative functions, putting little effort into fundamental societal changes such as integration of the various ethnic and regional groups into a solidly cohesive group (Fieldhouse 1966). Indeed, the imperial powers themselves had not yet attained national unification by the early twentieth century, as discussed above.

Minimal colonial administrations were sufficient to govern poor and fragmented colonies because they had imperial armies to back them up and because they made little attempt to develop the colonies or provide significant services. Upon independence, however, nascent governments immediately faced the expectation that they take on all the capacities of a modern state, ranging from defense to education to welfare programs. Problems associated with having a weak economy, minimal administrative capacity, and fragmented society were compounded by the much higher demands placed on newly independent sovereign regimes.

These difficulties of state construction are clearly demonstrated in recent examples of collapsed or failed states. States such as Somalia, Liberia, the Congo, and the Sudan were not functioning at even a minimal level during the 1990s and have been labeled as "collapsed" by Zartman and his colleagues (1995). Governmental structures hardly existed, and even the pretence of social or political order proved too taxing to maintain. Instead, bands of robbers and criminals roamed freely, terrorizing local people. Alexander Johnston noted: "In Liberia . . . the state has ceased to exist as a respectable member of international society, with even the façade of obligations to other states and its own people" (Johnston 1998:147). Another scholar observed that in many African countries "The tarmac roads have gone back to dirt roads, and the dirt roads in the countryside have ceased to be roads. Sewage, telephone, and electricity systems have long ceased to function" (Ng'ethe 1995:261). Yet paradoxically, these states remained sovereign members of the international system. In some sense, these states may be thought of as "permanently failing organizations"—states that no longer functioned, but were not allowed to cease existing (Meyer and Zucker 1989). Instead, failed states have been supported by the international system despite their obvious lack of qualification for state-hood, and most have been held up through international aid.

The Deceptions of Sovereignty

Although many recently independent states are unable to face the triple challenges of lack of governmental organization, lack of resources, and lack of national integration, one of the substantial resources available to weak states has been the support of the international community. The international community has validated the sovereignty of these states despite their lack of functional capabilities, and has even provided material resources in the form of development aid to maintain some level of governmental capacity (Jackson 1990). This support of the international system sustains the contemporary ecology of states, in which weak states continue on despite little *de facto* sovereignty or control.

In the contemporary world, the international community has gone to great lengths to support the sovereignty of weak states, effectively conferring the status of sovereignty on them *de jure* even when *de facto* sovereignty is absent. Weak states are granted privileges denoting sovereign equality in matters such as diplomatic recognition and an equal vote in the United Nations (Badie 2000). As Robert Jackson has noted: "Ramshackle states today are not open invitations for unsolicited external intervention. They are not allowed to disappear juridically—even if for all intents and purposes they have already fallen or been pulled down in fact" (Jackson 1990:23). Historically, the international community had taken a rather difference stance toward weak or disorganized territories. Most commonly, such regions were incorporated through territorial expansion or colonial domination. However, the collapse of states today has not resulted in recolonization or annexation that might bring resolution to endemic disorganization or conflict. Instead, weak states persist, as do their civil wars, perpetuating the contemporary ecology of states.

Additionally, the international community has provided large amounts of development aid, both state-based and funded by international organizations such as the World Bank and the International Monetary Fund. Bertram Badie has pointed out that this international development aid significantly contributes to perpetuating the illusion that weak states conform to the ideal state despite varying degrees of dysfunction, labeling these efforts the "deceptions of sovereignty" (Badie 2000:37). Badie argues that world polity institutions have created "deception" by camouflaging the reality of economic dependence of newly independent states and the weakness of their political structures, thus producing an erroneous picture of serviceable statehood (Badie 2000:131–2).

For states that are incapable of maintaining the reality of sovereign statehood, these deceptions are necessary to claim the status of a state. Weak states enact statehood by holding a seat in the United Nations, participating in summits and dialogues held by international organizations, and in general presenting the appearance of a functioning state. The international community supports this façade by providing substantial resources, both material and moral. Behind the façade, however, the state may lack the capability to fulfill the implied promises made to maintain order and control within its designated territorial borders.

Cyprus is an extreme example of a state that does not empirically fit the definition of a sovereign state. Since the ceasefire of its civil war in 1974, Cyprus has in reality been an island with two governments. The southern government, recognized as the legitimate government of Cyprus by the world polity, controls only half of the island. The northern half of the island, for all practical purposes, is governed by the Turkish Republic of Northern Cyprus (Minahan 1995). Inhabitants of the northern part of Cyprus pay taxes to, abide by the laws of, and accept the decisions of the northern government (Attalides 1979). But the international system only recognizes the southern government of Cyprus, even though that government does not have control over the entire island. Moreover, only the southern government is allowed to send representatives to the United Nations, sign treaties, and receive development aid from the World Bank and other banks. As one scholar notes without sarcasm: "The Government of Cyprus, which now only controls 60% of the area of the island, has not, by the mere fact of occupation, lost international recognition" (Attalides 1979:187).

In order to understand contemporary civil wars, it is necessary to acknowledge the fundamental weakness of state structures in many states, despite their appearance of robust sovereignty. The example of Somalia illustrates how the challenges of state-building, coupled with the demands of a modern nation-state, created the conditions for protracted civil war.

Somalia as a Weak State

Like many recently independent states, Somalia has not yet resolved the structural problems that it confronted when it became independent in 1960. Somalia's struggles for territorial integration are reminiscent of the historic difficulties England faced in the incorporation of Scotland and Ireland, or France's difficulties in the incorporation of Brittany. Somalia, however, lacked the resources possessed by these European states. Impoverished in natural resources and lacking a robust economy, Somalia managed to survive primarily by its reliance upon international aid. When civil war broke out in 1982, international aid proved insufficient to quell the uprising, and so the war escalated. Somalia's civil war raged for nearly a decade, at horrible cost to the civilian population. The consequences of the civil war and the withdrawal of international aid in the early 1990s led to the demise of that country as a functioning state.

Somalia was typical of a weak state in its lack of a coherent state structure and absence of material resources. The structural fragmentation of the Somali state was a relic of the circumstances of its independence, which required the unification of two separate colonial administrative structures. Before independence, the Somali people were divided amongst several different colonies, including Italian Somalia, British Somaliland, and Ethiopia, each under a different imperial power (Brogan 1998). Following Italy's defeat in World War II, Italy agreed to prepare its colony, Italian Somalia, for independence in 1960. In a surprise move, Britain also decided hastily to grant independence to its colony, British Somaliland, only three months before the independence of Italian Somalia. This would allow the two parts of Somalia to be united as a single country (Laitin and Samatar 1987).

Although the Somali people were delighted to be united, integration created serious challenges and inequities in the new state. Neither colony had been prepared economically or politically for independence. Instead, both had been characterized by "a condition of neglect and marginality" as colonies (Laitin and Samatar 1987:61). The northern, British half of Somalia had been less economically developed than the southern, Italian half. On the political front, nearly all of the work on the preparation of the constitution had been completed by Italian Somalia before Britain decided to allow the independence of its half of Somalia. Thus the northern British half of Somalia had little say in the new political structure and resented the dominance of the southern Italian half in setting the political agenda (Laitin and Samatar 1987).

In addition to economic and political inequalities, the bureaucratic integration of Somalia posed a major challenge. As remnants of their recent colonial past, each half of Somalia had its own judicial system, currency, administrative rules, taxation rates, accounting systems, and legal histories, which somehow had to be unified into a single system (Laitin and Samatar 1987; Lewis 1988). The problem of deciding upon an official language illustrates the significant structural heterogeneity of the new Somalia as well as its extreme cultural homogeneity. Nearly all of the citizens of the new Republic spoke Somali, a linguistic homogeneity that was quite unusual for a newly independent state. Somali was not a written language, however, so the government was faced with the option of creating a written Somali language and teaching it to everybody, or choosing one of the colonial languages of English or Italian. Since the decision was politically fraught, it was postponed and the new republic floundered for a decade without an official language. The educational system and government bureaucracy were forced to operate in three different languages (Laitin and Samatar 1987). This created serious problems of communication, as one might imagine, since civil servants within the government were frequently unable to communicate with each other without the aid of English-Italian translators (Lewis 1988). Gradually English became the *de facto* language of government and education, disadvantaging the Italian-speaking Somali of the south, and creating new resentments between the northerners and southerners (Laitin and Samatar 1987).

Somalia also faced the standard quandary of lack of resources. As one observer noted, Somalia confronted "a depressing future as a perpetually impoverished Third World country with very few natural resources, constantly burdened by drought and the refugees from Ethiopia" (Brogan 1998:99). To the extent that Somalia did function as a state, this may be attributed to massive amounts of international support. At independence, both Italy and Britain recognized that neither half of Somalia, much less both together, was economically viable. Both former colonial powers pledged large amounts of money and other types of aid to help Somalia in its early years (Lewis 1988). After independence, Somalia received military and development aid from a wide variety of sources, including the United States, the Soviet Union, China, the European Economic Community, the World Bank, and the United Nations. Somalia joined the Arab League in 1974, and thereafter benefited from the generosity of some of the OPEC countries as well (Adam 1995). Despite this aid, the outlook for Somalia was bleak. As one scholar commented: "It is astonishing that the new state worked as well as it did for its first 20 years" (Arnold 1995:427). When civil war broke out in 1982, predictably along the fault line of the former British half of Somalia and the former Italian half fighting each other, the weaknesses of the state were revealed in its inability to terminate the war.

The course of Somalia's civil war illustrates typical dynamics of the civil wars in weak states. The Somali government and armed forces lacked the capacity to contain the growing conflict, and did not possess the organizational and military capacity to conduct precision operations that might keep civilian casualties low. Somalia faced an all-too-common dilemma: allow insurgents to operate freely or engage in brutal tactics that would generate sympathy for rebels. Unable to root out insurgents, the Somali government adopted tactics in which entire cities held by opposition forces were bombed—flattened to rubble (Arnold 1995). While this tactic had a minor effect in quelling guerrilla operations, the effect on the civilian population was catastrophic. By 1990, the human rights group Africa Watch claimed that 50,000 civilians had been killed and 500,000 had fled due to the brutal tactics of the state (Arnold 1995). The massacres earned the Somali state widespread domestic and international unpopularity. Horrified by the killings, international backers such as the United States began to retract their support. Without international aid the government could not survive, and eventually collapsed in 1991 when President Siyad Barre fled the country.

As is typical in weak state civil wars however, the victorious rebel forces proved to be even more disorganized than the state had been. Rather than form a coherent movement united by a common leadership and a shared ideological vision, the various factions of the opposition coalition were prone to internal strife, with frequent quarrels among leaders. The opposition was composed of several groups, each controlling different territorial regions and attempting to control restive sub-groups with little coordination among groups. This lack of unity became particularly evident once "victory" was achieved. The rebel movement quickly dissolved into factions attacking each other. With no group strong enough to dominate the whole country, it fragmented into small feudal regions.

Following the end of the civil war, Somalia essentially ceased to function as a state, due in large part to the withdrawal of international aid (Adam 1995). Somalia's lack of ability to carry out the functions of statehood was extreme, qualifying it as a "failed" state—although again it is worth noticing that it still maintained the international status of a sovereign state. As one scholar wrote in 1995:

> The visible collapse of the Somali state has lasted half a decade. In some respects the country appears to have reverted to its status of the nineteenth century: no internationally recognized polity; no national administration exercising real authority; no formal legal system; no banking and insurance services; no telephone and postal system; no public service; no educational and reliable health system; no police and public security service; no electricity or piped water systems; weak officials serving on a voluntary basis surrounded by disruptive, violent bands of armed youths. (Adam 1995:78)

The extreme derangement of postwar Somalia was unusual even for a weak state, but its situation prior to the civil war in the 1980s is typical of a general pattern. The causes of Somalia's weaknesses were due to particular historical circumstances that resulted in structural fragmentation, disorder, and scarcity that are characteristic of weak states. As political scientist Joel Migdal has pointed out, recently independent states typically exhibit unexpectedly weak governmental structures composed of "disorganized, confused conglomerates of people and agencies," exhibiting "instability and ineptness" (Migdal 2001:59). These are the preconditions for lengthy civil conflict, of which Somalia's decade-long war is only one example.

Intractable Civil Wars in Weak States

Given the disorganization and fragmentation of weak states, it is not surprising that civil wars occur there. Yet the critical difference between strong states and weak states is in the duration of their civil wars rather than in their occurrence—civil wars in weak states last much longer. It is less evident why civil wars in weak states should last longer than in strong states. After all, one might imagine that a weak state would be easy to conquer with only a small but well-organized force, precisely because the state is already disordered and lacking in sufficient resources and governmental capacity to control insurgent groups. But it is the case that opposition forces in a weak state are typically at least as disorganized, if not more so, than the central state itself. The resulting weaknesses in both state structure and societal (rebel) organization tend to prolong civil wars.

Governments of strong states, in contrast, have much greater control over their societies, even in times of civil war. Strong states are typically able to contain their conflicts, preventing high levels of casualties and the geographic spread of conflict. Opposition groups in strong states are unable to act freely, are restricted in their access to weapons and targets, and members of the insurgency may be continually under threat of imprisonment or death. As a result, strong states are typically able to maintain social order in the parts of the country that are outside of the immediate rebel territory. Laws are enforced in areas outside the rebel territory, and the government continues to perform its normal functions. This is not to say that all is good within strong states. Often the control exerted by strong states is associated with significant human rights abuses. Yet for better or worse, strong states are usually able to repress insurgent groups sufficiently to prevent a protracted civil war.

Several factors work to prolong civil wars in weak states. First, weak states are not free from societal influences that undermine the ability of the government to negotiate in a trustworthy fashion and that discourage diplomatic solutions to civil war. Second, weak states lack the military capability necessary to root out opposition groups. Instead, they typically employ brutal, indiscriminate tactics—such as laying waste to whole villages in an effort to eliminate guerilla hideouts—that create sympathy for insurgents. Third, these states are often unable to control their territory and borders, often effectively ceding peripheral regions to insurgents as safe havens from which to base their attacks. Fourth, weak states often preside over similarly weak and fragmented societies. These societies produce disorganized and fragmented rebel groups that are often incapable of coordinated action and unable to abide by negotiated agreements.

Lack of Autonomous State Structure

One shortcoming that is quite common among weak states is the lack of an autonomous, rationalized bureaucratic structure that operates independently from local or kinship influences. In many weak states, government leaders are critically dependent on particular local groups, and are rapidly replaced—or even killed—if they act in a manner to displease those important constituencies. Lacking the ability to make independent decisions or compromises, governments may be unable to mollify opposition groups in order to avert or resolve civil conflict. These constraints on the ability of the government to negotiate and to carry out its promises have already been discussed in the literature on civil war termination, but scholars have failed to note the role of weak state structure in preventing trustworthy diplomacy (Walter 2002; Stedman et al. 2002; Fearon and Laitin 1996). In order to make sense of the inability of governments to make necessary concessions or keep their promises to rebel leaders, it is important to recognize the weaknesses of recently independent states.

Even in strong states, negotiations to end conflict may require a considerable amount of political courage and skillful diplomacy. Leaders in strong states may be prevented from making concessions owing to considerations of popular support and the desire to perform well in the next election. One explanation of the long U.S. presence in Vietnam, for instance, was that presidents were concerned that if their administration pulled the American troops out of Vietnam, their party would lose the next election (Kahin 1986). Great Britain faced a similar problem in negotiations over Northern Ireland (Kennedy-Pipe 1997). Even so, the worries of governments in strong states, typically over opinion ratings or the outcome of the next elections, pale in comparison to the concerns of governments in weak states.

Government leaders in weak states are forced to spend much of their energy protecting themselves from the constant risk of coups and over-throws—dangers that are much less prominent for leaders of strong states. Indeed, the government in a weak state is often as much in danger from its own constituents as from opposition groups. Unpopular negotiations with rebels can cause the downfall of a government nearly as easily as victory by insurgents. As a result, governments might not make the concessions necessary to placate the rebels; or if concessions are made, the government might not be able to carry out its promises to insurgents when threatened with the loss of public support.

The Sudan serves as an example in which the lack of state autonomy led to the resurgence of civil war. The termination of the first civil war in 1972 was attributed to the virtuoso negotiations of President al-Nimieri, in an example of brilliant statesmanship that temporarily overcame the structural limitations of state weakness. Eventually, however, the continuing weak state structure and over-dependence upon societal elites led to the onset of a second civil war in 1982. Accounts of the Sudanese civil war typically blame Nimieri personally for having gone back on his earlier promises and bowing to the demands of Islamic elders outside of the state. Instead of accepting this explanation, we may see the Sudan as a typical example of the difficulties weak and dependent governments face in negotiating in a trustworthy manner.

The first Sudanese civil war began in 1963, waged by the Anya-Nya guerrilla organization in southern Sudan. The war had been triggered by the introduction of governmental policies aimed at spreading Islam and the Arabic language in the non-Muslim black populations of southern Sudan (Arnold 1995). By 1972, however, President al-Nimieri had successfully negotiated an end to the war. Under the terms of the Addis Ababa agreement, the three southern provinces of Sudan were given regional autonomy in which most of the internal affairs of the region were to be controlled by a regional legislative assembly and executive (Arnold 1995). The Addis Ababa agreement was considered a great achievement, and has been considered a model for the mediation of other civil wars (Anderson 1999). As one historian summed up: "Nimieri's major concession was that Sudan should not be an Islamic republic; [in return] the south gave up talk of secession" (Arnold 1995:445). Glory for the civil war's resolution was laid at the feet of President Nimieri, and in 1974 it could be confidently stated that

"Southerners agreed that he was the first Northern leader who was keeping his promises to the South" (Eprile 1974:160).

Nevertheless the Sudan remained very weak and highly dependent on local groups for support. Nimieri's difficulties in consolidating and maintaining power forced him to defer to northern Islamic leaders, who insisted on Islamic fundamentalist rule. Without a sufficiently strong and rationalized governmental structure, Nimieri was unable to insulate the state from the demands of societal groups, represented in this case by Islamic leaders. In 1983, eleven years after the Addis Ababa agreement, Islamic (Sharia) law was introduced throughout the Sudan along with new regional arrangements that reduced southern autonomy. These violations of the Addis Ababa agreement and the imposition of Islamic law throughout the country enraged the southerners. A second civil war broke out, initiated by a group calling itself the Anya-Nya 2 (O'Ballance 2000). Although frequently described as the result of Nimieri's villainous breaking of promises to the people of southern Sudan, this example better illustrates the reliance on the sanction of powerful societal elites that typifies the governments of weak states. Despite his concessions to Islamic elites, however, Nimieri was ousted in 1985 and his successors were unable to bring the civil war to an end despite multiple attempts at negotiation.

In sum, lack of autonomy undermines the ability of governments to treat opposition groups more fairly, as conciliatory policies may provoke outrage from majority domestic populations and risk the overthrow of the government. Governments are thus limited in the concessions they can offer rebels or may be forced to retract their promises in order to maintain the support of their constituents. In contrast, governments in strong states are better able to act independently of societal groups, and may lose an election but do not risk overthrow or civil rebellion.

Lack of Military Capability

Weak states typically lack sufficient military capability to limit rebel activities, due to insufficient economic resources and also to the lack of the kind of knowledge, skill, and experience that are required to carry out modern military maneuvers competently. On the one hand, the state typically fails to contain or root out insurgents. On the other hand, the lack of military capacity and effective control often leads to very high civilian casualties. The seemingly callous disregard for life by the government can create sympathy for rebels and escalate the civil war.

Citizens of strong states are used to highly effective police forces and, on occasions of greater turmoil, an almost pinpoint accuracy of military forces to hit targets while protecting bystanders. These high expectations are illustrated by the loud criticisms when these expectations are not met, as when U.S. planes accidentally bombed the Chinese embassy in Yugoslavia during the conflict over Kosovo (Jahn 1999). Such expectations are based upon the impressive level of organizational and military capabilities in strong states, which can be utilized to limit the scope of civil and interstate conflict. Domestic conflicts that erupt in strong states can be cordoned off, allowing daily life to continue in the rest of the country. For instance, during the thirty years of "troubles" in Northern Ireland, life in Great Britain continued more or less as usual beyond the Northern Irish counties under martial law (Kennedy-Pipe 1997). This type of cordoning can be accomplished in a strong state in part owing to superior resources and in part to highly effective governmental structures such as the police, the judiciary, and disciplined military forces. Moreover, the strong state often takes extreme pains to ensure that innocent civilians are not targeted in the attacks on rebel forces. Analogous to a police officer that allows a suspect to flee rather than shooting into a crowd of bystanders, the strong state may err on the side of civilian safety rather than the annihilation of rebel forces. Even then, innocent civilians may be killed despite the considerable organization and high-tech weaponry employed to preserve them. In a relative sense however, strong states are typically able to protect the majority of their populations even when fighting a civil conflict.

Weak states usually cannot suppress insurgents with such care. In many cases, weak states resort to tactics of all-out warfare that result in massive civilian casualties, substantial human rights abuses, and generation of greater sympathy for rebel causes. Lacking the military capability to make finer distinctions, weak states frequently resort to indiscriminate slaughter of guerrillas and civilians alike, in the hopes of controlling insurgents. The Somali civil war provides an example in which cities identified as succoring guerrilla forces were destroyed, killing thousands of people.

In El Salvador, for instance, the government-supported death squads

of the late 1970s were considered one of the main factors that contributed to popular support for the guerrillas. Twenty thousand deaths
were attributed to the death squads between 1980 and 1982, including
members of the legitimate opposition party, trade union organizers,
and Archbishop Romero, leading to widespread popular support for rebel forces (Brogan 1998). Once a new government had been installed
and the activity of the death squads curtailed in the mid-1980s, popular
support for the insurgents declined. As one observer noted, the "best
hope" for the revival of the insurgency would have been "that the new
Arena government would revive the deaths squads and its former policy of generalized massacre" (Brogan 1998:479). Instead, the lack of
popular support for the insurgency, coupled with the end of the Cold
War, led to the termination of the El Salvadoran civil war in 1991.

Governments of weak states may also simply be unable to control the
military. In Guatemala, for instance, the newly elected civilian president Marco Vinicio Cerezo Arévalo "found he was a prisoner of the
military with little room in which to embark on policies of which they
did not approve" (Arnold 1991:603). Without an effective hierarchy
of military command, state-sanctioned actions intended to suppress
insurgents may be taken as opportunities to carry out personal feuds
and to ransack property. Governments may lose control of their own
militaries once fighting has begun, and this usually leads to vicious
atrocities.

Although weak states commonly resort to brutal tactics, the result
is rarely a decisive victory. Widespread carnage frequently backfires
against the state, generating new recruits and popular support for the
opposition, while often having little effect on suppressing guerrillas
(Goodwin 2001). Moreover, as in the cases of El Salvador, Guatemala
and Somalia, reports of atrocities may cause withdrawal of international aid and support, further weakening the government's ability to
carry on the civil war.

Lack of Territorial Control

Many newly independent states are so weak that they effectively cede
peripheral geographic areas to rebels, who then gain a safe haven for
local supporters and recruits, safe bases, and lines of supply. This lack
of territorial control is partly a consequence of insufficient governmen-

tal and military power, but colonial history and geography also play an important role. In many cases, it is not so much that opposition groups have wrested territory from the government, but rather that peripheral regions were never really integrated into the nation-state in the first place. Insurgents may be operating from strongholds that the government had never penetrated, supported by locals who had never recognized the legitimacy of the new state. This situation presents greater challenges to a state compared with simply regaining territory that it has lost to rebel forces.

Strong states rarely have regions in which rebels can function beyond the control of the government. Even in countries as territorially large as Canada, the United States, and China, there are virtually no areas that lie beyond the reach of the state. Strong states also tend to effectively monitor and control border crossings to bases in a neighboring country, and are capable of mustering diplomatic muscle and/or military force if necessary in order to close borders with neighbors. Thus there is often no place in a strong state where rebel groups can organize free from state vigilance and harassment. Rebels may engage in opportunistic attacks or terrorism, but usually cannot sustain a large-scale war or conquer significant territory.

In contrast, although the weak state is granted jurisdiction over its entire territory by the international system, it often lacks functional control of outlying regions beyond the capital city. As a result, the weak state may be unable to prevent rebel groups from building bases in peripheral areas, allowing a variety of options for guerrillas. One possibility is that the state may virtually cede peripheral regions of the country to the insurgents, maintaining state control only in the capital and surrounding areas. Alternatively, rebels may set up bases just over the border in a neighboring country, creating a haven that is somewhat, although not entirely, protected by the norms of sovereignty. In addition, weak states are often unable to stop transfers of weapons and supplies across territorial borders, allowing intervening states to provide material support and training for opposition forces.

Guerillas operating in weak states frequently take advantage of peripheral regions of the country to train new recruits, rearm and regroup, and to provide bases for forays that harass the neighboring countryside. For instance, Fidel Castro and his guerrillas retreated to the safety of the Sierra Maestra mountains following multiple defeats by the Cuban army (Clodfelter 1992). Each time the rebels were able to hide and rebuild their strength, until they eventually succeeded in overthrowing the government in 1959. The civil war fought by the Shining Path for over ten years in Peru provides another example. The Shining Path guerrillas were based in the region of Ayacucho, a rural area that had historically received little governmental attention and control. Much of the success of the Shining Path has been attributed to the lack of any kind of organization in Ayacucho, governmental or otherwise. As an editor of a Peruvian news magazine stated: "There has traditionally been no government presence in many areas [of Ayacucho] . . . Hence . . . there are no liberated areas, only abandoned areas" (Marks 1996:261). The Shining Path had much greater difficulty penetrating areas beyond Ayacucho that had local grassroots organizations and more significant state presence (Berg 1994).

When borders are loosely controlled, insurgent groups can slip out of the country and get weapons and supplies to slip in. Rebel groups frequently take advantage of the lack of border control to create relatively safe camps in neighboring countries for training and recruitment. Arms shipments from neighboring countries are also a major source of strength for opposition groups. For instance, in Liberia, neighboring West African countries provided much support for opposition groups. Charles Taylor, the leader of the insurgent group that eventually took over the government of Liberia, was assisted by Libya, Burkina Faso, and the Ivory Coast from which he received military supplies (Lowenkopf 1995). Taylor was also aided by international businesses in the United States and Europe, which paid $9 million a month into his funds in exchange for raw materials such as iron ore, rubber, timber, diamonds, and gold, indirectly contributing to the purchase of arms and supplies (Lowenkopf 1995). The role of external actors in supplying, training, and funding opposition groups is a critical piece in the puzzle of the lengthiness of civil wars—one that builds upon the inability of the weak state to control its own borders.

Finally, it is important to note that civil wars place extreme burdens on already weak states. Even in times of peace, weak states frequently do not exercise authority over peripheral regions or adequately patrol borders; governmental control may be limited primarily to the capital city and nearby regions. In times of civil war, these failures of authority can be greatly exacerbated, providing opportunities that strengthen the opposition and prolong the war.

Lack of Cohesion and Organization of the Opposition

In strong states not only is the state well organized and supplied with resources, but so also are societal groups. The scholarly literature on civil society emphasizes the important role played in strong states by societal sectors outside the government (Seligman 1992; Putnam 1993). In contrast, civil society and social organization can be extremely underdeveloped in weak states. In weak states the government not only provides the major locus of political organization, but is also the key actor in economic and societal organization. Beyond the government, societal organizations in weak states tend to be scattered, disorganized, and fragmented in both civilian and rebel contexts. I use the term "patchwork coalitions" to depict the fragmentation and disorganization characteristic of insurgent groups in weak states.

The patchwork coalitions that typically form the opposition in civil wars reflect a general lack of social organization and coherence. Rather than forming a tightly organized body with a cohesive set of leaders, these patchwork coalitions are frequently composed of coalitions of groups that may agree on their distaste for the existing government but disagree on all else. These coalitions may differ in their composition, their tactics, and their vision of the future, making negotiations between a unified opposition front and the state impossible. This lack of cohesion is often a key factor prolonging the civil war, as different factions will dispute amongst themselves on the war aims, preventing a negotiated end to the conflict or even unified agreement to a truce. In addition, should the opposition front defeat the state, civil war may recur as the illusion of unity dissolves and various factions of the opposition begin to fight each other.

It is common for various factions within the opposition coalition to favor radically different goals. For instance, in Myanmar, which has experienced civil war since its independence in 1948, the patchwork coalition is composed of a variety of groups with startlingly different goals. One of the major groups of the coalition is the Communist Party, whose goal has been control of the government and the establishment of a communist system. Another longstanding opponent of the government has been the Karen ethnic group, which demands complete autonomy and independence from the state. The Shan people make up yet another piece of the patchwork, an ethnic group that possesses quite heterogeneous goals even amongst themselves. Rival

Shan groups coexist uneasily, and some are more concerned with operating their illegal businesses in drugs or smuggling than in the political
goals of independence and autonomy. Other groups in Myanmar—the
Arakans, Mons, Karennis, Kachins, Palaungs, Pa-Os, and Was—also
have grievances against the state and have joined the patchwork coalition at various times since independence (Arnold 1991).

This disagreement among the factions on the goals of the civil war
provides a formidable obstacle to negotiation, as a settlement that might
placate one group will fail, almost necessarily in the case of Myanmar,
to satisfy others. The government of Myanmar made some concessions
and offered amnesty to guerrillas in 1980, successfully appeasing some
rebels, though other factions remained belligerent. For instance, the
Karen still demanded the creation of an independent Karen state
(Minahan 1995). Since no set of concessions could placate all of the rebels, the civil war has continued as one of the longest minority conflicts
in post-World War II history (Gurr et al. 2002).

Not only is negotiation difficult when opposition groups are fragmented, but victory does not ensure future peace. Even if the opposition defeats the state, it is common for civil wars to continue as various
factions of the opposition group fight amongst themselves for control
of the government. Angola provides one example, although cases such
as Somalia and Chad might serve equally well. Prior to 1975, indigenous Angolan groups appeared to be united in their goal of achieving
independence from Portugal, despite the multiplicity of leaders and
ideologies within the opposition coalition. After the Portuguese withdrawal in 1975, however, the disunity among the various groups of
the opposition became evident as intense fighting broke out amongst
them. Three major groups are commonly identified as the combatants
in the civil war that lasted from 1975 to 1991, although splinter groups
also emerged and re-merged in this period. Eventually, a settlement
was reached between two of the groups in 1991. The third group, under Jonas Savimba, refused to abide by the terms of the settlement and
continued fighting for several more years (Brogan 1998). While united
in their resistance to Portuguese imperialism, the subsequent decades-
long civil war illustrates the fundamental lack of a shared vision of the
future within the opposition.

In sum, not only the state is weak but often also the opposition can
be characterized as weak in being substantially disorganized and frag-

mented, lacking a unified command hierarchy with leaders that have the legitimacy and the power to make and enforce decisions. Members of the patchwork coalition squabble among themselves, unable to control their own members and negotiate on behalf of themselves or other factions. In contrast, in civil wars where decision-makers exist on both sides, civil wars are more likely to be short and decisive.

The Downward Spiral of Weak States

The situation of weak states does not admit an easy solution. Civil wars have been difficult to terminate successfully because the structural factors that maintain them are persistent and resist quick repair. Moreover, weak states that have already experienced civil wars are likely to become even weaker. Civil wars further de-legitimate the authority of the state, increase popular distrust of the state system, use up resources, and polarize politics. These conditions create a downward spiral that increases the likelihood of civil wars to recur in weak states. It may be that recently independent states that were able to sidestep civil war in their early decades have had an opportunity to build stronger governmental and military structures and develop experience that will contribute to a greater capacity to end swiftly any civil wars that start in the future. Weak states that have experienced lengthy civil war, however, may find it even more challenging to establish strong, legitimate state structures in future decades.

Given that it is extremely difficult to strengthen war-stricken states, hopes for improvement may have to come from other sources. The solution to the civil wars in weak states might lie not in strengthening states, but in the development of alternate channels of political action that bypass the state. The European Union is an example of a supranational organization in which individual and group rights are recognized. Arguably, this has resulted in decreased tension between subnationalist groups and their states, as in the case of the Basques in Spain (Lynch 1996; Conant 2001). To the extent that individual citizens and political groups are able to appeal directly to international organizations for political protection, economic gains, and social welfare, the incentives in wresting these goods from the state through civil war might diminish. Powerful international institutions of that sort do not exist at present. But there are hints of such structures in the rapid expansion of transnational mobilization on issues such as human rights, democracy, indigenous rights, and so on (see Meyer et al. 1997). The expansion of such institutional structures of the world polity may eventually serve to dampen civil conflict.

Unfortunately, weak state structures are not the only conditions that increase the length of civil wars: the perils of the Cold War and the potent effects of interstate intervention have also contributed to recent civil conflicts. Ethnicity, which has been so emphasized in the media and elsewhere, is also frequently cited as a source of strife. However, as we shall see, ethnic dynamics prove less crucial than weakness of the state in accounting for the length of civil war.

4

Ethnic Conflict in Weak States

RATHER THAN FOCUS on the weaknesses of the state to account for the nature of contemporary civil war, many contemporary observers have taken a different approach, turning to concepts such as ethnicity and identity to make sense of these conflicts. Scholars have posited that the potent solidarity of ethnic opposition groups results in lengthier and more intractable civil wars. Similar logics have been extended to other group identities such as religion, language, region, culture, or to groups bound together by shared grievances of oppression and discrimination. Although the particulars of these claims differ, their similarity lies in the proposition that features of the warring groups, such as their identities, culture, or historical grievances, account for the distinctiveness and intractability of civil wars.

I argue instead that the structural characteristics of the state and the society in which the civil war takes place are more influential for the length of the civil war than the particular identities or attributes of the groups fighting the civil war. Neither ethnic nor nonethnic groups are likely to engage in civil war in strong states, due to their structural factors. Strong states offer opportunities for nonviolent political change as well as formidable obstacles for any group attempting violent resistance. Conversely, both ethnic and nonethnic groups are likely to wage civil war in a weak state. Put simply, lengthy civil wars tend to occur in weak states rather than in strong states in the contemporary period, regardless of ethnicities, identities, cultures, or grievances.

Although I reject the notion that ethnicity and identity can explain lengthy and intractable civil wars, there is no doubt that ethnic and identity-based groups are prominent in some civil wars. I argue that this, too, is often a consequence of weak states. In the absence of strong political institutions, political mobilization occurs around social groups rooted in ethnicity, religion, or geography. Such groups form the basis of normal politics in a weak state, fighting over standard political goals such as access to resources and political inclusion.

Identity-based explanations for lengthy civil war contain some flawed assumptions. First, the common view that identity-based groups are unusually cohesive and unified is empirically problematic, and so is the presumption that ethnic or identity-based groups foster a distinctive type of conflict. As a result of these problems in the literature, the conceptual category of ethnic war has evolved into a "miscellaneous" category for any conflicts that do not fit the image of the prototypical European civil war. As political scientist Kurt Gantzel (1997:123) comments: "Violent conflicts which *prima facie* are not conflicts between states, social classes, interest groups or political parties" are now fashionably labeled "ethnic war." Although scholars have provided little theoretical or empirical evidence to support the distinction of the "ethnic" civil war, this concept persists as a blanket explanation for wars outside of the Western ken.

The near absence of ethnic or identity-based civil wars in strong states, despite the presence of many discontented ethnic minorities, provides a starting point for my claim that weak states, rather than ethnicity and identity, lead to lengthy civil wars. I also argue against the commonly held notion that identity-based groups engaged in armed conflicts are particularly cohesive and homogeneous, and that they are distinctive from other kinds of groups that might wage civil war. The 1960s civil war in the Congo provides an empirical illustration of the limitations of identity-based arguments. Finally, I argue that those aspects of civil war that have been taken as indicators of ethnic or identity-based politics can be understood as ordinary political processes common to many structurally weak states.

A note on nomenclature: a bewildering array of labels has arisen for groups under the rubric of ethnic conflict. Although ethnic groups per se comprise only a small number of groups involved in contemporary political conflicts, scholars have broadened the category of ethnic conflict to include "minorities" (Gurr and Harff 1994), "ethno-religious" groups (Fox 1999), or simply "identity-based" groups (Kaldor 1999). This proliferation of labels has unfortunately occurred without careful consideration of which groups should be included and excluded from the category of ethnic conflict. As a result, nearly every war in the Third World could be included in the category of "ethnic" conflict (and probably has been, at one time or another). In this work I tend to use the broad term of "identity" in order to emphasize the common basis of these explanations. At times I use the terms "ethnicity" or "minority" group instead of "identity-based" groups—but the general argument developed here is not limited to these sub-categories.

Identity-based Conflicts in Strong States

The critical importance of state structures quickly becomes apparent when one compares identity-based conflicts in the stronger states of the West with those in recently independent weak states. Strong states have no shortage of groups bound by shared ethnicity, religion, culture, or language. One can think of a host of examples in the United States, Canada, Great Britain, Spain, France, and other countries. Moreover, identity-based groups in strong states often engage in political conflict. But these groups have rarely waged large-scale civil wars—instead pursuing less violent tactics such as protests and demonstrations—because of the potent military and governance structures that are common to strong states.

The absence of identity-based civil wars is not for lack of minority grievances. The strong states of the West have a long and shameful history of oppressing minority groups. The history of the indigenous peoples in the Americas, the hardships of the descendents of African slaves, and the unhappy lives of many immigrant groups demonstrate that ethnic and minority mistreatment is not limited to the recently independent states of the Third World. Sadly, strong states tend to be even more effective than weak states in carrying out policies of ethnic discrimination, given their greater governmental and military capabilities. Minority groups in strong states are also typically better organized and more vocal than ethnic groups in weaker states (Olzak and Tsutsui 1998). In sum, identity groups with potent grievances can be found in abundance in strong states.

One indicator of the prevalence of identity groups with grievances in Western states is the number of groups identified in the Minorities at Risk dataset, which is currently one of the most widely used datasets of minority or identity-based conflicts (Gurr and Harff 1994). It provides a comprehensive list of all conflicts since 1945 that have involved minority groups, ranging in intensity from nonviolent political protests to high-casualty civil wars. Many of these groups are located in Western states, including ethnic mobilizations in Quebec, Northern Ireland, and Chechnya. Indeed, the Minorities at Risk dataset shows that nearly twenty percent of the identity-based groups in the world engaged in political conflict are located in Western states, supporting the perception that there is no shortage of identity-based groups in strong states.

At the same time, few minority or identity-based groups in strong states have waged high-casualty civil wars. For instance, between 1945 and 1995, none of the groups in Western Europe or North America listed in the Minorities at Risk dataset met the Correlates of War criteria of one thousand deaths in a civil conflict. In contrast, the Minorities at Risk dataset listed forty states in the Third World that were engaged in minority-based civil wars involving at least a thousand casualties. It seems unlikely that the scarcity of minority-based civil wars in strong states is due to a paucity of identities or grievances in these states.

I argue that the absence of protracted, high-casualty civil wars in strong states is due to the differential capabilities of strong states compared to weak states, rather than the particular identities or attributes of the groups involved. Although strong states are not immune to identity-based civil wars, they typically experience political protest and rioting rather than outright civil war. In contrast, weak states are often unable to prevent their riots and insurgencies from escalating into full-scale civil wars. This inability is owing to their lack of resources and institutional bureaucratic structures, however, rather than to more intense ethnic passions in weak states.

Strong states are able to prevent their ethnic—as well as their non-ethnic—insurgencies from erupting into large-scale civil war in several ways. First, their governmental structures can ameliorate minority grievances. Strong states possess institutionalized political systems that can deal with grievances and provide channels for political change. As Olzak and Tsutsui (1998) have argued, these political channels for addressing minority grievances provide an important alternative to violent rebellion. For instance, oppressed ethnic groups in the United States have been able to gain increased recognition through institutionalized political processes of legislating and judicial decisions. Similarly, the province of Quebec in Canada held a referendum on secession, obviating the need for an armed uprising (Young 1999). While these channels may not work as satisfactorily as minority groups might wish, they are far more effective than their analogues in weak and disorganized states—and strong states are much more likely to be able to hold up their side of the bargains that they strike.

Second, strong states have substantial military capabilities that can be used to control minority rebellions by coercion. Police and military forces are able to subdue rebels while keeping casualties among innocent bystanders to a minimum. Violence is generally prevented from spreading beyond a tightly controlled area, allowing daily life to continue normally throughout most of the country. Strong states such as Great Britain and Israel have been able to contain civil unrest to relatively localized areas of the country, in part through the harsh application of policing techniques such as martial law, arrests, and surveillance. Although these strategies are imperfect and innocent bystanders may be harmed on occasion, these techniques have generally been effective in preventing the escalation of these minority protests into high-casualty civil wars.

These abilities of strong states to utilize coercion should not be assumed to imply a benevolent state, but can result in substantial human rights abuses and political repression. China, for instance, subdued Tibet through the use of brutal tactics that have been frowned upon by the international community (Brogan 1998). Russia has received widespread international criticism for the human rights abuses that have occurred as a result of its attempts to control the Chechen insurgency, which also represents one of the few contemporary cases of large-scale minority or identity-based civil war in a strong state (SIPRI 1995–2000).

I suggest, therefore, that the relative infrequency of identity- or minority-based civil wars in strong states cannot be attributed to the weakness of identity groups in these states or a lack of motivating grievances. Instead, the relative absence of ethnic civil wars is due to the coercive and institutional means utilized by strong states to reduce the scope of ethnic rebellions. Weak states, in contrast, are frequently

unable to wield sufficient governmental and military power to effectively either assuage or repress minority groups. The difference between strong and weak states lies, therefore, not in the use of repressive
tactics by the state, but in the capacity of the state to wield those tactics
effectively.

Identity-based Explanations of Ethnic Conflict

It is commonly believed that ethnic conflict has increased explosively
since the end of the Cold War (Cornell 2002; Sadowski 1998). As interstate conflict has waned, concern over ethnic conflict has correspondingly waxed. In the words of one scholar: "animosity among ethnic
groups is beginning to rival the spread of nuclear weapons as the most
serious threat to peace that the world faces" (Maynes 1993:5). Not only
are ethnic conflicts posited as more virulent than conventional civil
wars, they are believed to be harder to resolve. Ethnic enmities are
painted as fiercer than pale political antagonisms, leading to more intractable conflicts than civil wars that are politically motivated. This
way of conceptualizing the ethnic conflict has some serious problems.
One is the assumption that ethnic groups are dangerous because of the
unusual strength of ethnic ties. Likewise, ethnic conflicts are assumed
to differ in a fundamental way from conventional civil wars. Neither of
these claims has been supported by systematic empirical evidence.

Identity Groups as Cohesive and Homogeneous

Much of the persuasiveness of ethnic or identity explanations derives
from the assumption that identity-based groups are especially cohesive,
determined, and unified. For instance, Chaim Kaufmann (1996:138)
writes that "the key difference" between ethnic civil wars and those
based upon political ideology is "the flexibility of individual loyalties,
which are quite fluid in ideological conflicts, but almost completely
rigid in ethnic wars." Stephen M. Saideman (2001:23) claims that "ethnic identity, by its nature, creates feelings of loyalty, interest, and fears
of extinction" that distinguish ethnic identities and conflicts from those
based on other identities. Yet few identity-based opposition groups empirically exhibit these characteristics of cohesion and solidarity. Instead, opposition groups in weak states tend towards fragmentation

and disunity as a result of the patchwork nature of the coalition, re-gardless of the particular identity upon which they have mobilized.

Scholars of ethnic identity have provided a great deal of evidence that identities are neither fixed nor fundamental, varying instead over time, by circumstance, and even within a given individual (Barth 1969; Gans 1999; Cornell and Hartmann 1998; Nagel 1982; Eller and Coughlan 1993). In addition, identities are typically multiple, overlapping, and hierarchical. As a result, an opposition group that is mobilized on the basis of ethnicity may still have substantial cleavages based on other differences. The multiplicity of identities contributes to the patchwork effect, as homogeneous ethnic groups are typically divided by class, religion, culture, language, geography, or other sources of identity.

For instance, James Manor (1996) points out that at least four types of identities have been politically salient in India: (1) religious identities, (2) linguistic identities, (3) geographic or sub-regional identities, and (4) caste-like or tribal identities such as the "scheduled tribes" of India. Each identity is quite significant in its own right, and a potential vehicle for collective mobilization. However, these identities do not necessarily correspond neatly with each other; instead, each individual is located in a maze of multidimensional and overlapping identities. Moreover, political attention shifts from emphasizing one set of identities to another. In one election geographic identities might be dominant. In another election class, caste, or language might be mobilized, leading to different configurations of the electorate (Manor 1996). Indeed, Manor notes that on one occasion, when Indian political boundaries were redrawn so that one sub-region was dominated by a single linguistic group, "they discovered all of the things that divided them—caste, class, religious, sub-regional, urban/rural, and other factors" (Manor 1996:466). The multiplicity of identities, in India and elsewhere, makes the creation of a truly homogeneous opposition front unlikely. Instead, groups unified on one dimension tend to splinter on the basis of conflicting sub-identities.

This multiplicity of identities is typical of opposition groups in weak states. Donald Horowitz (2000) has argued that the scale of modern states and civil wars frequently requires that political identities be built from amalgamations of smaller groups that vary in their ethnic identities, languages, or other characteristics—resulting in patchwork coalitions. Often a single ethnic, linguistic, or other identity group is simply too small numerically to figure in national politics—perhaps numbering in the hundreds rather than in the hundreds of thousands. These small identity groups commonly band together in order to have enough individuals to wage a large-scale civil war. While such amalgamations may be unified along one particular dimension, such as religion or geography, the coalition is likely to be differentiated along other dimensions, such as ethnicity or historical experience, promoting a tendency towards disorganization and fragmentation. As a result, factional infighting and splintering often characterizes these opposition fronts.

The civil war in Somalia illustrates the fragmented and patchwork nature of identity groups in weak states. Even seemingly homogeneous groups possess cleavages that can result in fragmentation and even war. Somalia is unusually ethnically homogeneous, and ethnic divisions were not at the root of its conflict. Nearly 97 percent of the population is Somali, generating the claim that Somalia is "Africa's sole indigenous nation-state" (Johnston 1998:138; Minority Rights Group 1990). Indeed, the unification of Italian Somalia and British Somaliland was a victory of ethnic unification over arbitrary colonial borders—an achievement thought to eliminate the possibility of civil conflict. Alexander Johnston notes that in Somalia, unlike in other countries of Africa and even of Europe, "all the people . . . share a common tradition. They speak the same language, respond to the same poetry, derive their wisdom (and their experience) from the camel economy, and worship the same god" (Johnston 1998:138).

And yet, as he sadly concluded in light of the devastating civil war in Somalia, "clearly, the absence of ethnic divisions has counted for very little" (Johnston 1998:138). Although the people seemed unified on the basis of ethnicity, language, religion and culture, these similarities were overridden by differences in colonial experience and geography. The civil war in Somalia was fought by the north against the south as a consequence of political interests and the legacy of colonial divisions (see Chapter 3). The original unification of British and Italian Somalia was based on the assumption that similarities of ethnicity and culture would prove to be of greater importance than the cleavages produced by the administrative separation of the colonies. That assumption proved incorrect in the context of a weak state, as shared ethnicity and language did not ensure unity in Somalia. The lesson is clear: if an ethnically homogeneous nation in a weak state can easily fragment and collapse, the same is likely to be true of other identity-based opposition groups.

Few opposition groups fit the image of a homogeneous group that is substantially more cohesive and determined than ordinary groups, such as political parties. Opposition groups in weak states tend to be patch-work coalitions that derive from fragmented societies, composed of a variety of ethnic or religious subgroups with quite different goals and hopes for the future. Such groups may marshal claims on the basis of their collective identities and grievances—sometimes putatively rooted in the ancient past. But these groups contain many cleavages. They tend to fall apart fairly easily, and may turn on each other after victory. If ethnic or identity-based groups are no more cohesive than other op-position groups, there is no basis for assuming that identity-based con-flicts will be distinctive—either lengthier or more bitter—than other types of civil wars. This forms the basis for a second criticism, below.

The Distinctiveness of Identity-based Conflicts

Ethnic and identity-based issues are widely accepted in both academic and popular thinking as an explanation for contemporary civil wars. Yet few scholars have tried to justify why ethnic conflicts should be consid-ered analytically distinct from other forms of civil war. Little attention has been paid to examining whether identity-based groups and their grievances are substantively different from other kinds of social groups. The failure to address this issue results from the absence of any clear basis for determining which conflicts should be considered ethnic or identity-based and which should not. The labels "ethnicity" and "iden-tity" have been applied so casually that the concepts are nearly useless from an analytic standpoint. Furthermore, the ethnic-conflict litera-ture as a whole has committed the sin of "selection on the dependent variable" in which only cases where ethnic identities are deemed to have led to conflict are studied. This severely limits the conclusions one may draw about such conflicts.

The concept of identity-based conflict has become so broad that it has lost its utility as an analytic category. Although sociologists have defined ethnic groups as those based upon a "subjective belief in com-mon descent" (Weber 1968:389), the category of identity-based con-flict has been broadened to include religious, linguistic, or regional groups, those with shared cultural values or historical experiences, or any minority that has suffered from discrimination (Gurr and Harff 1994). Thus the concept of identity-based conflicts seems to cover civil wars of every possible stripe. For instance, Mary Kaldor defines "identity politics" as "the claim to power on the basis of a particular identity—be it national, clan, religious or linguistic" (Kaldor 1999:6–7). She does not stop there, but also includes political identities such as communists, democrats, monarchists, and republicans as identity groups that have historically engaged in "identity politics" (Kaldor 1999:6–7). The liberality with which the identity label has been applied to conflicts makes the concept nearly useless for analytic purposes.

As a result, one cannot reasonably identify cases of identity-based conflicts, or compare them to conflicts of any other type. Indeed, it is nearly impossible to imagine a conflict that is not rooted in some sort of collective identity. Nor does the literature provide guidance for excluding groups from the identity-based category. In practice, groups in strong states based on political parties seem to escape the identity label. All the same, there seems no justification why party-based groups should not also be conceptualized as identities—and indeed Kaldor argues that they should be included under the umbrella of identity politics. If there is no clear theoretical basis for designating conflicts as other than identity-based, it becomes impossible to design a study that tests whether identity-based conflicts are distinctive in any manner.

The tendency of the media (and some scholarly work) to characterize civil wars in weak states as founded on ethnic or identity-based hatreds, while portraying civil wars in strong states as political or ideological, may reflect a Western-centric bias. Virtually all civil wars could be characterized as rooted in conflicting identity groups, but it is those in the Third World that tend to be labeled as such, often with implications that such conflicts are irrational, inevitable, or even barbaric. In contrast, the civil wars in Western history are often represented as sober disagreements over alternative visions of the state. The simplistic labeling of civil wars as identity-based or "ethnic" may reflect a cultural bias, and thus may not always prove the most useful analytical approach for scholarly analysis.

The second problem with the ethnic/identity-based conflict literature is the tendency of scholars to select on the dependent variable, choosing only cases where identity-based conflict was the outcome.

Researchers in this tradition have examined identity-based conflict with the *a priori* assumption that they are cases of a special type of conflict, but provide little justification for this assumption. Crucial comparisons to identity-based groups that did not engage in conflict, or to conflicts not involving identity-based groups, have not been performed. As a result, the inferences that can be drawn from case studies are seriously limited. Many ethnic wars are bloody and long—but that in itself does not support the conclusion that ethnicity *caused* the conflicts to be bloody or protracted. After all, many nonethnic wars are also long and bloody. Without appropriate comparisons, it is impossible to assess the distinctiveness of identity-based conflicts, whether in their lengthiness, casualties, dynamics, or intractability. As a result, scholarly literature has failed to recognize that many aspects attributed to ethnicity or identities are, in fact, quite common in weak-state civil wars.

The labels of ethnic conflict and identity-based conflict stand, therefore, without sufficient justification of their merit as analytic categories. It is possible that future studies will show that ethnic or identity-based conflicts are distinctive in some way from other conflicts. Currently, however, the distinctiveness of identity-based conflict has not yet been established and should not be assumed. Indeed, when ethnic groups have mobilized politically in Western states such as Canada, the United States, or in Latin America, they have used political strategies such as petitions, marches, demonstrations, and voting power that are commonly used by all sorts of political groups, rather than engage in some distinctively ethnic type of political action. Similarly, civil wars waged by identity-based groups look very similar to other civil wars in weak states. Although the content of the identities or issues of every conflict are locally situated and unique, these particulars may not affect the course of the resulting civil war. In sum, the importance or relevance of ethnicity or other identities in civil wars does not necessarily imply a unique form of politics or conflict.

The Congo is a fairly typical example of a war that has been considered to feature ethnic politics. In this as in other cases, the identity-based groups turned out to be far from homogeneous. Instead, the course of the war was driven by straightforward political processes rather than by unique ethnic identities or ancient hatreds. Understanding the way in which the opposition identities and grievances were developed may provide insight into the particular issues and discourses of the war. Knowing that identity-based groups were involved, however, does not explain much about the way the Congolese civil war unfolded, or why it lasted as long as it did.

Ethnic Conflict in the Congo

This section examines the role that ethnicity and identity played in the 1960s civil war in the Congo (formerly Zaire). This war is commonly labeled as an ethnic conflict: thus, for example, it was included in the Minorities at Risk dataset as a "minority" conflict involving the Luba and Lunda minority groups (Gurr 1994). The Congo is also discussed as a case of "ethnic polarization" by Crawford Young (1976), who asserted that "no analysis of the emerging political system in the Congo can escape grappling with the elusive problem of 'tribalism,' or ethnicity" (Young 1965:232). When examined closely, however, the Congolese civil war did not feature a homogeneous and cohesive ethnic opposition, but was instead an example of a multiethnic coalition linked by common geography and economic concerns. While understanding the particular identities involved does provide a sense of the specific grievances, it does not explain much about the dynamics of the civil war. Instead, the length and character of the Congolese civil war can better be explained by the opportunities presented by the weakness of the newly independent state combined with the influence of the Cold War and substantial interstate intervention.

Knowing only that the Congolese civil war was triggered by the attempted secession of the Katanga region and that it is generally considered an ethnic conflict, one might be forgiven for imagining that the Congolese civil war featured a single ethnic group, presumably the Katangan people, united in their desire to create a homogeneous nation-state that was ethnically and culturally distinct from the rest of the Congo. In actuality, the Katangan rebellion was fought by a geographically defined coalition of multiple ethnic groups connected by economic interests, rather than a single group united by ethnic bonds.

Katanga was an administrative province (akin to a U.S. state or Canadian province) that Belgium had treated as a colony separate from the rest of the Congo until 1930 (Young 1965). Several different ethnic groups lived in Katanga, including the Lunda, Bayeke, Basanga,

Tshokwe, Batabwa, Babemba, and the Baluba (Gerard-Libois 1966). Upon independence in 1960, these diverse ethnic groups mobilized in support of regional secession, claiming to be protecting the rights of "authentic Katangans," by which they meant the inhabitants of the administrative region rather than a specific ethnic group. Although mobilized on the basis of a common region, historical experience, and set of economic concerns, the coalition was far from internally cohesive, as evidenced by internal struggles and disagreements that eventually resulted in the withdrawal of the Baluba (Saideman 2001).

The "strangers" encroaching upon "authentic Katangans" were not a unified ethnic group either. Instead, they were immigrants from the neighboring Congolese administrative region of Kasai, a region that was also composed of various ethnic groups including the Lulua and Baluba. The immigrants from Kasai did not invade Katanga as a unified front with a common identity, but came individually, searching for a place to live. Historians claim that the basis of the conflict lay in the fears of Katangan residents that the immigrants from Kasai would snatch away jobs and land in Katanga because the Kasai residents were more educated and possibly more favored by the government (Gerard-Libois 1966). These fears were real but of recent origin, as they primarily became relevant with the transition to statehood.

While ethnic explanations tend to focus upon the identities and history of the groups involved, as for the Katangan coalition, they often fail to pay attention to the structure of the state in which the civil war took place. In the case of the Congolese civil war, the attempted Katanga secession occurred immediately after the Congo had declared independence, and moreover, it was not the only problem the new government faced that month. A mutiny of the army had been in progress for a week when the two richest provinces, Katanga and Kivu, both declared secession nearly simultaneously (Brogan 1998). By the end of 1960, the Congo had splintered into four fragments. Two regions claimed to have seceded, while of the other two each claimed to be the legitimate capital of the Congo (Weisburd 1997).

This splintering and fragmentation of the newly independent Congo was based on fundamental structural weaknesses inherited from the Congo's colonial legacy. Belgium, the colonial power, had done almost nothing to prepare the Congo for independence. As Crawford Young described it, "Total colonialism was replaced by total independence virtually overnight" (Young 1965:572). The state structure was "virtually improvis[ed] from scratch," and was essentially a replica of the Belgian constitution that had been revised for the Congo only five months previously (Young 1965:56). Hence the Congo had almost no practical experience in the workings of its newly created political institutions before independence was declared.

In addition to its lack of state structure, the Congo suffered from the structural challenges of its geography. It is the third-largest country in Africa, populated by over 200 ethnic groups and administratively divided into six provinces (Arnold 1991). At the time of independence, each of the six provincial capitals was nearly completely isolated from the others, with no roads connecting them, and the two main cities were located at opposite ends of the country and linked more closely to neighboring countries than to each other (Young 1965). These structural weaknesses, plus the lack of governmental capacity, the lack of geographic cohesion, and the lack of an established political system, made fragmentation in the form of secessionist attempts likely, regardless of the strength of ethnic ties.

The Congolese civil war lasted four years. The duration of the war can be attributed in great part to the weakness of the newly independent Congolese state. The constitutional framework of the government collapsed in the midst of the war, less than three months after independence (Young 1965). Additionally, the Cold War and substantial international intervention importantly contributed to lengthening the Congolese civil war. The ethnic or identity relations of the Congo, in contrast, provide a poor explanation for the duration of the civil war or its dynamics.

Politics and "Identities" in Weak States

Whether or not ethnicity or identity is causally implicated in the course of civil wars, it does appear that ethnicity and identity groups often play a role in politics and conflicts in the Third World. Does this reflect the potency of ethnic/identity-based bonds? Or is the political presence of ethnic and identity-based groups also a consequence of structurally weak states? I suggest that the centrality of identity-based groups in politics is neither driven by primordial ethnic hatreds nor mysteriously potent identities, but rather is a byproduct of normal politics in weak states.

Politics in weak states operates somewhat differently than politics in strong states. However, these differences should not be mistaken as indicating particularly strong identities and passions. I discuss three characteristics of identity politics in weak states: (1) the prevalence of identity-based groups in politics, (2) the development of grievances or discrimination around identity-based groups, and (3) the existence of nationalist goals. Each has been viewed as evidence of the importance of ethnicity and identity. I will argue, in contrast, that each is driven by the ordinary politics of weak states.

I propose that the lack of institutionalized political identities in weak states leads to politics that are carried out by groups mobilized along existing social and cultural identities such as ethnicity. Likewise, the prevalence of claims of ethnic discrimination in weak states results from political controversies over inclusion and exclusion that bedevil all states and need not be taken as an indicator of longstanding ethnic hatreds. Ethnic nationalist rhetorics are common among weak states, and do not necessarily reflect strong expressions of ethnic solidarity. In short, the political salience of identity-based groups is the result of structurally weak states.

Political Participation by Identity-based Groups

The presence of ethnic or other minority groups in the political sphere is often assumed to reveal the overriding power of ethnic or identity-based ties. I offer an alternate view: the political salience of ethnic identities results from the absence of institutionalized political identities in weak states. Political party identities in weak states are typically quite undeveloped and often exert little influence. As a result, normal politics in weak states revolves around other social or cultural identities that are rooted in societal or organizational structures—such as religious groups, ethnic groups, and so on. The presence of ethnic and other minority groups in the political arena can thus be seen as the workings of normal politics in weak states, rather than potent identities that override more rational political affiliations.

One of the distinctive capacities of strong states is their ability to establish political identities that meaningfully shape participation and issues in the political arena. As a result, civil wars in strong states are often fought between clearly delineated and well-organized political parties, say Liberals against Conservatives, or perhaps between ideological

political movements such as communists contending against democrats. Ethnic groups have gained power and prominence in recent decades as important interest groups in these strong states. Even so, this
increased power is usually reflected in the incorporation of minority
interests into mainstream parties—such as the wooing of minority
groups by both Republicans and Democrats in the United States—
rather than by the founding of new political parties that wholly correspond to ethnic identities. Thus political parties in strong states stand
independent from other identities such as ethnicity, religion, or geography.

In contrast, political identities in weak states tend to be underdeveloped and may even be brand new. In the example of the Congo, political parties had barely come into existence before the first elections
were held (Young 1965). As a result of their newness, political parties in
weak states frequently do not provide a basis for the structuring of political identities and behavior. Instead, politics in recently independent
weak states have tended to organize around preexisting social identities, including ethnic but also religious, geographic, cultural, linguistic,
or historical identities. The particular social identity that becomes politically salient depends upon the nature of society before independence. These social identities do not represent a distinctive form of political behavior, but instead act much in the way political parties would
if they were sufficiently well organized to structure political life.

It is not the case that ethnic passions override more rational identities based on political platforms and party allegiances in weak state
politics. Instead, political groups in weak states tend to be grounded in
ethnic, religious, or other social identities because institutionalized political identities have not yet been developed. Ethnic politics in weak
states is simply politics and does not imply strong or ancient passions
and hatreds. Consequently, political conflict based in ethnic or minority identities does not necessarily lead to a different type of civil war
compared to those fought by political or class-based identities in weak
states.

Identity-based Grievances of Discrimination

The media is fond of portraying identity-based grievances as resulting
from ancient enmities that reach back into the mists of time. For in-

stance, Robert Kaplan, in an *Atlantic Monthly* article on the Balkan wars, muses: "The various popular convulsions in the Balkans are inexorably converging on Macedonia, just as they were doing a century ago" (Kaplan 1991:104). Students of ethnic conflicts have convincingly disputed this claim of ancient hatreds. As Jack Snyder (2000:18) points out, "Most of the globe's recent strife is not due to ancient cultural hatreds . . . Serbs and Croats, for example, never fought each other until the twentieth century." Indeed, grievances of group discrimination are usually contemporary in origin. I extend these arguments to propose the following: minority grievances of discrimination are a common currency of political struggle rather than a uniquely ethnic or identity-based form of politics.

Not only are identity-based grievances and discrimination rarely "ancient" in origin, but it is not clear that they should lead to longer or more bloody wars compared with the grievances of class-based groups, political minorities, or any other type of group. Throughout history, political and class-based groups have experienced harsh discrimination and often respond by starting insurgencies, much like the conflicts of identity-based groups. Grievances built around discrimination and issues of political incorporation are a common currency of political struggle, rather than something distinctive of ethnic and identity-based groups alone.

Conflict over who is included and who is excluded from political participation is one of the primary loci of political struggle in both strong and weak states (Schattschneider 1960). In various countries in Latin America, for instance, civil wars in the nineteenth century were commonly rooted in struggles over shares of government power between the Liberal and the Conservative parties (Clodfelter 1992). Strong states have historically held passionate debates that sometimes erupted into violence over who was allowed to vote, receive the rights of citizenship, and count as a member of the political polity. These debates on political inclusion continue in strong states to the present day and should be seen as fundamental to the workings of the politics in strong states generally.

Similarly, questions of political inclusion and discrimination form an important basis for political conflicts in weak states. Indeed, weak states may be even more likely than strong states to enact discriminatory policies owing to government dependence on societal elites. Governments in weak states must rely heavily upon the support of societal elites to maintain power. This reliance on societal elites introduces weakness into the state by preventing the development of bureaucratic structures that are insulated from kinship or local ties. Weak governments are then forced to incorporate "localistic orientations" into their policies, which may manifest as favoritism towards one group, identified by ethnicity or other social indicators such as religion, geography, language, or culture (Skowronek 1982). The necessary outcome of favoritism towards one group, however, results in bias and discrimination against other societal groups. The resulting discriminatory policies can therefore be understood as a general phenomenon resulting from the inability of the weak state to resist pressures from powerful social groups that are pushing for privileges for themselves. As in the case of Yugoslavia, however, they can be seen as a consequence of present-day struggles for political power rather than as rooted in longstanding ethnic hatreds (Kunovich and Hodson 1999).

Sri Lanka provides one example of a moderately strong state that was still unable to resist social pressures to enact discriminatory policies, which later set off an intractable and bloody civil war. In that country about 74 percent of the population is Sinhalese (speaking Sinhala), while 18 percent is Tamil and 7 percent is Muslim (Rotberg 1999). After its independence in 1948, a Tamil government was elected in the first three elections. Despite being in the minority, the Tamils held most government posts at the time of independence because of their fluency in English when Sri Lanka (Ceylon) was a British colony (Little 1994). In 1956, Sinhalese presidential candidate Solomon Bandaranaike decided to run on a "Sinhala language only" platform to appeal to the majority of voters who were Sinhalese (Rotberg 1999). The success of this ploy, which resulted in Bandaranaike's electoral victory, led to discriminatory policies against the Tamils, which fueled the civil war to come.

The election of Bandaranaike, based on his discriminatory language platform, is a typical form of political opportunism rather than an indication of deep ethnic hatreds. The enactment of discriminatory policies against the Tamils was particularly likely in a weak state such as Sri Lanka, which was dependent upon the Sinhalese majority and unable to resist Sinhalese pressures for access to government posts and other privileges. The more general characterization of an election that appealed to the interests of one set of constituents over another is certainly not limited to ethnic contestants alone. Further, the resulting civil war need not rest solely on the identity-based nature of Tamil grievances; it can be seen as consequent on a combination of factors, including a government dependent on its Sinhalese constituents, the fragmented nature of the Tamil opposition, and significant interstate intervention.

The puzzle of weak states is not why groups with grievances exist, but how groups that have been historically discriminated against economically, politically, or culturally can still muster the resources to prosecute a full-scale civil war that lasts for many years. In part, the answer lies in the weakness of the state, which allows even weak opposition groups to successfully mobilize and wage war. In addition, discriminated groups in contemporary times are often aided by interstate interventions that provide essential resources (see Chapter 6). These arguments, which apply to weak states generally, imply that contemporary civil wars can be distinguished neither by the strength of the grievances that motivate them nor by the uniqueness of the identities that participate in them. Instead, the distinctive characteristic of the post-World War II period has been the prevalence of weak states that not only perpetrate discrimination, but also lack the capability to effectively suppress the resulting uprisings.

Ethnic Nationalist Goals

Demands for national autonomy or separatism are often taken as an indicator of the uniquely ethnic character of civil wars. According to Anthony Smith, "Given the chance, most ethnic movements in Africa and Asia would opt for outright separatism" (Smith 1981:138). Another scholar notes: "Most ethnic conflicts in recent times have been fueled by a group's bid for greater autonomy, full national independence, or affiliation with a neighboring country" (Callahan 1998:23). These nationalist claims are usually assumed to reflect the aims of a cohesive and unified ethnic community. As I argued previously, however, opposition coalitions in weak states are often fragmented and fundamentally divided, featuring multiple identity groups and diverse aims. In these cases, the opposition may agree only on a common dislike of the incumbent government and disagree on all else. In these circumstances, nationalist rhetorics serve as a kind of "lowest common denominator" of the various goals and ambitions of a patchwork coalition.

Explanations of ethnic nationalism are typically rooted in the assumption that the ethnic or cultural group is a cohesive and homogeneous community with consensus on preferred political structures and policies. From this perspective, ethnic groups are conceptualized as monolithic, with internal rules and customs that are incompatible with those of the larger society around them. For instance, Michael Hechter assumes there is a fundamental political incompatibility between a homogeneous ethnic nation and its government, when he argues that, all things being equal, an ethnic nation "would prefer to be sovereign rather than ruled by another nation" (Hechter 2000:116). This picture of nationalism in which an ethnically homogeneous community demands sovereignty may reflect the European experience of the nineteenth century, but does not accurately portray the disorganized politics of minority communities that characterize weak states today. Indeed, scholars have even questioned whether the nationalism of nineteenth-century Europe represented a homogeneous community, implying that the nationalist prototype might not be an accurate depiction of either historical or contemporary reality (Calhoun 1995; Hobsbawm 1990).

Empirical cases of contemporary civil war in weak states rarely feature ethnic opposition groups that are homogeneous, unified, and cohesive. As one scholar points out: "Ethnic groups are the least institutionalized of political groups; that is, they have little formal organizational structure, standard procedures, or central coordination" (Marshall 1997:88). It is common for civil wars to feature multiethnic or nonethnic coalitions linked by convenience rather than brotherhood, as was the case in the Congo. Even within a single ethnic group, as in Somalia, social cleavages of class, religion, region, or other divisions can lead to rifts within the group.

These divisions result in fragmented opposition groups, which are liable to have quite different and often irreconcilable ambitions. Fragmented opposition groups in weak states may demand autonomy and self-government, but these claims should not be assumed to represent the unified wishes of a cohesive ethnic community. While every member of the opposition may (or may not) have a grievance against the state, the particular content of those grievances and the envisioned recompense can disagree considerably. Separatist claims can serve as a kind of "lowest common denominator" of the multiple and possibly conflicting goals held by different factions of the opposition. National- ist demands for independence may thus be understood as a general antistate rhetoric in many cases, rather than a true representation of ethnic solidarity.

Nationalist claims might also be doubted as the true expression of opposition goals, because in several empirical cases separation has not provided the promised end to nationalist conflicts. Nicholas Sambanis (2002) reminds us that separation and partition did not resolve conflicts in Croatia/Serbia, Ethiopia/Eritrea, India/Pakistan, and the northern and southern halves of Somalia, but only led to further conflict. The continuation of conflict is puzzling in these cases if we take the declara- tions of nationalism as authentic representations of the collective will of a homogeneous ethnic and cultural community. Conversely, if we understand these separatist demands as a "lowest common denomina- tor" antistate rhetoric that served to unite a fragmented and disorga- nized opposition coalition, it is much less surprising that the coalition dissolved and internal wrangling began once the goal of independence had been attained.

For instance, the Moro civil war that began in the Philippines in 1972 (and still continues into the twenty-first century) has generally been considered a separatist conflict even though some of the opposi- tion sub-groups favored nationalist goals while others did not. The Moro identity is based upon commonalities in geography and religion, which provide the basis for the creation of a common identity for Mus- lims who are concentrated on the southern islands of Mindanao and the Sulu archipelago (Brogan 1998). Within the Moro front, however, ethnic and cultural differences are evident, as thirteen different ethno- cultural groups are amalgamated into the composite Moro identity (Che Man 1990). Moreover, the Moro are indistinguishable racially and linguistically from other Filipino groups. The principal grievance of the Moro is not based on previous experiences of state repression or injustice. Instead, their chief concern is reportedly that they "fear being swamped in a Christian flood" as Christian settlers from Luzon have settled in traditionally Moro areas, a position similar to the fears of the inhabitants of Katanga in the Congo (Brogan 1998:242).

This heterogeneity of identity groups that coexist under the um- brella of the Moro identity is reflected in the diversity of opposition aims in the civil war. Although the conflict is generally termed "separatist" (Gurr and Harff 1994; Minahan 1995), the Moro groups disagreed to a considerable extent on their war aims. Indeed, disunity among the groups has been a major aspect of the conflict. For four of the five major Moro groups, the goals of the civil war ranged from greater regional autonomy to full independence and statehood (Che Man 1990). The most radical faction of the Moro did aim to create an independent nation-state, but the other three groups were more concerned with negotiating greater autonomy with the Philippine government. The fifth group held a significantly different aim, hoping to make the Philippines an Islamic state, and explicitly did not desire to create an independent state (Che Man 1990). As only one of the five major groups claimed national independence as a goal, it is questionable whether the "separatist" label should be applied to the Moro civil war as a whole. But nationalist claims did serve to provide a semblance of unity among the fragmented groups of the Moro opposition, even though these claims should not necessarily be taken at face value as an authentic expression of Islamic nationalism or ethnic solidarity.

As the example of the Moro suggests, the diversity of aims that can be embodied in a patchwork coalition implies that concessions that might satisfy some members of the opposition are unlikely to satisfy others. After all, how much autonomy will suffice to end the conflict, when even complete independence might not be adequate for the faction that hopes to make the Philippines an Islamic state? Although the government of the Philippines has satisfied some Moro leaders by allowing greater regional autonomy to Moro districts, low-intensity fighting has continued because other groups with different goals remain unappeased. This outcome is typical in weak states. Civil wars are often prolonged because the lack of rebel consensus on war aims prevents successful negotiation, even when governments are willing to grant concessions. Claims to greater autonomy, the particulars left unspecified, may suffice to unite disparate groups in order to begin a war, but governmental concessions of greater autonomy are rarely sufficient to end the war.

Ethnic Conflict Reconsidered

I have argued that civil wars in weak states are driven by the disorganization of the opposition, coupled with deficiencies in the governmental and military capabilities of the state, rather than by the particular identification of the groups involved. Identity-based groups mobilize in strong states, but rarely instigate civil war because of the availability of other avenues for political change and unwillingness to confront the military strength of the state. Identity-based groups in weak states find far fewer options for nonviolent political change. As a result, these groups are more likely to turn to civil war as a means of instituting change.

The civil wars fought by identity-based groups in weak states do not appear to be different in their dynamics or intractability from civil wars fought by more conventional class- or politically based groups in these states. In addition, I have suggested that those aspects of civil wars that have been attributed to their identity-based nature, such as the participation of identity-based groups, grievances of experiences of discrimination and oppression, and nationalist claims, are actually expressions of normal politics in weak states, rather than of identity-based groups specifically. Thus the greater frequency of lengthy civil wars and "ethnic politics" in weak states is due to the military and governmental incapacities of the state rather than the attributes of the identity-based group itself.

The argument presented in this chapter challenges scholars of ethnic conflict to clarify and defend the uniqueness of the territory they have staked out. As one writer has complained, "the term ethnic conflict has become a euphemism for substate conflicts we cannot explain or comprehend" (Marshall 1997:82). It is not valid simply to assume that ethnic conflict and "identity politics" are necessarily distinct and deserving of study in isolation from other types of civil conflict. Instead, students of ethnic conflict must provide theoretical arguments and empirical demonstrations of the distinctiveness of the dynamics of identity politics in civil wars in order to justify the analytical uniqueness of their domain.

5

The Effects of the Cold War

SCHOLARS HAVE BRANDED many Third World civil wars as "proxy wars"—conflicts that were an expression of the larger Cold War hostilities between the United States and the Soviet Union (Gaddis 1997; George and Smoke 1974). Thus it seems uncontroversial to claim that the interstate rivalry of the Cold War affected civil wars of the period. Yet analysts have failed to address one important issue: why were the superpowers so concerned with civil wars in the Third World? After all, weak, recently independent states were unlikely to make a significant military contribution if a world war were to break out between the superpowers. The attention paid to the political commitments of weak states in the Cold War was unusual from a historical standpoint. Previous rivalries between powerful states did not typically extend to conflicts of peripheral states, but remained centered on the primary quarreling parties (Frederick 1999; Black 1999). Upon reflection, it is surprising that these peripheral states, which ought to have been militarily and strategically irrelevant to the Cold War, gained so much attention and resources from the superpowers.

An explanation for how and why the Cold War lengthened civil wars in the post-1945 period is due. Arguments of the Cold War have traditionally fallen under the jurisdiction of political realists, but the effects of the Cold War on weak-state civil wars cannot be understood as the necessary outcome of a Great Power rivalry. Instead, its cognitive and ideological aspects were the essential factors. In the first place, the conceptual framework shared by Cold War participants rendered the political stances and alignment of weak states relevant to the interests of the superpowers. The ideological focus of the Cold War and its particular emphasis on recruitment of allies focused attention on the recently independent weak states that had not yet aligned themselves with one side or the other.

At the same time, the ambiguous and murky politics of some weak states offered interpretive flexibility—affecting whether superpowers viewed conflicts as relevant to the Cold War or not. Accounts of Cold War conflicts in U.S. textbooks rarely question whether or not the label of a pro- or anticommunist struggle was accurate. When one examines the historical record more closely, however, the distinctions of "communist" and "pro-Western" become much more ambiguous. In many cases the perception of ideological commitment was developed from foggy indicators of the stances of various government officials and sharpened only as a regime began clearly to side with (or garner support from) one of the superpowers.

These two processes proved highly consequential for the length and intractability of civil wars in the Cold War era. Once internal fighting was interpreted as a Cold War conflict, the cognitive and material resources of the superpowers and their allies were critical in lengthening civil wars. This argument is consistent with the political realist perspective, which argues that the bipolar world structure encouraged superpower intervention in Third World states (Waltz 1979; Gilpin 1981). Here I draw attention to the conceptual processes that preceded superpower decisions to intervene, without assuming that the relevance of weak state civil wars to superpower interests was necessary and obvious. Many of the examples below discuss the interpretations and judgments of the United States rather than the Soviet Union. This bias reflects the greater availability of close historical studies of the role of the United States in Cold War conflicts. Histories of Soviet interventions are still in short supply in the West.

Discussion of the cognitive frames of the Cold War, which led to an emphasis on ally recruitment (Snow and Benford 1988), will next lead me to analyze the interpretive processes that labeled specific conflicts as relevant to the Cold War. Communist insurgencies in Guatemala and the Philippines will be used as examples to highlight the interpretive processes involved. Next, I examine the effects of the cognitive and military resources on the length of civil wars. I find that Cold War processes lengthened at least thirty of the civil wars fought since 1945 and in several cases prevented their resolution until the end of the Cold War itself. Finally, I briefly consider recent arguments that Islam represents a new ideological bloc with the potential to generate a new cold war.

Understandings of the Cold War

Cold War theories and cognitive frames had serious implications for those civil wars deemed by superpowers as relevant to their strategic interests. States that wavered in their allegiance to the West, particularly those in Central America, were frequently compelled to adopt a more pro-Western stance, whether by diplomatic pressure or by force (Booth and Walker 1999). Likewise, states that faltered in their commitment to the communist cause, such as Hungary and Czechoslovakia, were similarly pressured by Soviet tanks and military battalions (Porter 1984). Weak states around the world were pegged by Soviet and American planners as falling into one camp or another. The perceived importance of these peripheral states in the superpower struggle derived, most obviously, from the idea of fundamental incompatibility of the two competing and highly legitimated models of the state, so states had to choose one side or another. The superpowers and other international actors shared theories of ally recruitment, and often worked from the assumption that Third World states were pawns in the expansionism and counterexpansionism of the superpowers.

Ideological Models of the State

Neo-institutional theorists point out that the structure and behavior of states can be greatly influenced by exogenous norms, "blueprints" or models drawn from the broader international community (Meyer et al. 1997; Suchman and Eyre 1992; Thomas et al. 1987). In general, though, neo-institutionalists presume—or at least have primarily studied—circumstances in which there is substantial international consensus (Meyer et al. 1997; Suchman and Eyre 1992). In rare historical moments, however, the international community has supported two or more *alternate* and competing models of the state. The Cold War was one such moment, in which two highly legitimated alternatives existed, a circumstance that paved the way for both intellectual and military combat.

Following World War II, the Western and Soviet models offered alternate visions of the ideal state. Both models were strongly legitimated by powerful constituencies in the international community, and both had evolved into potent ideologies. In periods when only one model of the state is supported by the world polity, that model typically becomes taken for granted and is widely adopted. When two legitimate models of the state are available, however, actors must choose. Moreover, in the case of the Cold War, both models advanced strong ideological claims that the other form was fundamentally incompatible. Whereas in historical perspective one can imagine (and find concrete historical examples of) hybrid forms, the general consensus was that each state could only be on one side of the conflict. In short, each model claimed to be the sole legitimate model of the state.

The existence of two polarized and highly legitimated models in the world polity can lead to bitter civil conflict within nation-states. Both sides sustain strong ideological beliefs in the justness of their cause—a view that is bolstered by the support of many, although not all, members of the international community. Even if one side in a civil war commands the situation militarily, the opposition is likely to retain its belief in the fundamental rightness of its position and may be less likely to yield. One might think of the situation as analogous to a war in which the opponents both believed they were fighting on the side of God, a frequent occurrence in the seventeenth century (Bendix 1978). When both sides are convinced they are following the Right cause, neither is likely to back down, and conflict is likely to be particularly fierce and intractable.

The Recruitment of Cold War Allies

The international Cold War consensus further presumed the expansionary nature of both sides—which encouraged and justified superpower intervention in Third World conflicts. Previous Great Power rivalries did not assume such an expansionary character, and thus remained focused more directly around the core opponents. For instance, the arms race between Britain and Germany at the turn of the twentieth century did not involve peripheral countries, nor did the historical competition between Britain and France for supremacy in European continental politics (Frederick 1999; Black 1999). The Cold War, on the other hand, evolved to become a war of ally recruitment. Although the two superpowers built up their own arsenals, much of their efforts lay in preventing the subversion of one or another of their Third World allies to the other camp. Once a communist or pro-Western regime had been established, the other camp tended to cease attempts to remove or alter it using military force, instead redirecting energy to prevent other dominoes from falling (Graebner 2000). The ill-fated Bay of Pigs was one of the few attempts by the United States to convert a communist state back to the Western fold. Such interventions were relatively feeble, given the strength of the superpower that lay behind the effort. Political realists have interpreted this reluctance as resulting from the effectiveness of deterrence policies.

This strong emphasis on recruiting allies only makes sense if one takes into account a critical shared assumption in the Cold War milieu: not only were opposing sides expansionary, but they were monolithic. The Soviet Union assumed that a victory by a pro-communist leader represented a victory for communism everywhere. As John Lewis Gaddis notes, there was "little strategic logic" in providing aid to the Castro regime because Cuba was essentially indefensible by the Soviet Union. Ideologically, however, "Cuba was all-important: it might provide the spark that would set off Marxist uprisings throughout Latin America" (Gaddis 1997:290–291). Thus the Cuban revolution was seen by both the Soviets and Americans as support for the theorem that communism was expansionary, even though the likelihood of successful revolution in the rest of Latin America was unrealistic. The assumption of monolithic nature became a self-fulfilling prophecy when Castro's Cuba was immediately supported by the Soviet Union and repudiated by the United States.

U.S. policymakers in the 1950s and 1960s believed not only that all communist revolutions would support the Soviet Union, but that all nascent communist movements were actually orchestrated by Moscow—a belief that does not hold up to empirical scrutiny today, but fit with the theories of the times. In the 1950s political theorists and government officials envisioned that the entire Third World might eventually succumb to communism, which in turn would automatically result in Soviet world domination (Arnold 1955). For instance, a 1948 National Security Council study (NSC-7) stated: "The ultimate objective of Soviet-directed world communism is the domination of the world. To this end, Soviet-directed world communism employs against its victims in opportunistic coordination the complementary instruments of Soviet aggressive pressure from without and militant revolutionary subversion from within" (cited in Graebner 2000:28). Richard Barnet sums up the early Cold War position of the United States:

> The essence of the argument is that guerrillas in Vietnam, Thailand, Peru, Guatemala, and Angola are all part of the same army. If the army can be defeated in Vietnam, it will not be necessary to fight it in Thailand or the Philippines. If the insurgencies are not opposed, that will demonstrate a lack of resolve, just as Munich did, and eventually the guerrillas will challenge the U.S. directly and then we will have to fight World War III to defend our homes and honor. (Barnet 1968:273)

Moreover, the United States feared that communism was an insidious force that could subvert whole nations even without direct military invasion from the Soviet Union. U.S. policymakers had concluded by 1946 that the Soviet Union was unlikely to extend itself militarily for some time (Graebner 2000). Nevertheless, the United States feared the power of communism was so overwhelming as to be able to convert Third World countries without a fight. Robert McNamara wrote how, in 1961, the Kennedy administration feared that "a metaphorical 'extension cord' reaching all the way from Moscow (believed to be the true source of power) to communist Pathet Lao forces in Laos by way of Beijing and Hanoi" would bring about the fall of Laos to communism. Extending the logic developed during the preceding Eisenhower administration, policymakers concluded that if Laos fell, "it would be just a matter of time until South Vietnam, Cambodia, Thailand and Burma would collapse" (cited in McNamara et al. 1999:29).

As early as the Truman administration, U.S. policymakers began to imagine elaborate chains, such that the loss of Greece to Communism would lead to the conversion of Turkey, then the Middle East, France, Western Europe, Northern Africa, and finally Asia and South America

(Graebner 2000). In his memorandum on Turkey in 1946, Acting Secretary of State Dean Acheson wrote:

> If the Soviet Union succeeds in its objective of obtaining control over Turkey, it will be extremely difficult, if not impossible, to prevent the Soviet Union from obtaining control over Greece and over the whole Near and Middle East . . . [including] the territory lying between the Mediterranean and India. When the Soviet Union has once obtained full mastery of this territory . . . it will be in a much stronger position to obtain its objectives in India and China. (cited in Graebner 2000:21)

This reasoning made sense only if one assumed that communism was monolithic, and that support for communism equaled support for the Soviet Union—assumptions that would be shown to be incorrect in future years. If policymakers did not automatically equate communism with "those allied with the Warsaw Pact," there would have been little reason for the United States to intervene in peripheral countries around the world. Yet I do not mean to imply that these fears were mere figments of the imagination and hence groundless. Both superpowers and their interstate allies firmly believed in the assumptions of the Cold War, including the necessity of ally recruitment and the theories of containment and deterrence. These beliefs were highly consequential. If the United States had given up its efforts to sway Third World regimes, the Soviet Union might indeed have won under these particular rules of the game. As Cold War historian John Lewis Gaddis sums up:

> It is easy now to sit back and say that the United States and its allies never had much to worry about in the "third world"—that there was *no* prospect that Marxism-Leninism would catch on there. But the failure of fears to materialize does not establish their immateriality. Revolutionary ideologies have indeed, in the past, spread widely: none more so than the American example of 1776 . . . Nightmares always *seem* real at the time—even if, in the clear light of dawn, a little ridiculous (Gaddis 1982:187–8).

The shared understanding among members of the international community that there were two monolithic and competing models of the state drove subsequent efforts to intervene in civil wars throughout the Third World.

The Interpretation of Communist Influence

Cold War controversies usually center on debates over strategy—which actions the superpowers ought to have taken. Less examined is the more fundamental question of whether superpowers correctly identified regimes as communist or pro-Western. Determining the ideological leanings of a state in the world of the Cold War was not as simple as might appear at first glance. In some cases a state might have strategically declared itself to be allied with one side or the other of the Cold War, in the hopes of gaining development aid and possibly military support to fight domestic insurgents. In other cases the superpowers attempted to deduce the ideological stance of a government, a job that was especially tricky given the murky politics and patchwork coalitions of recently independent weak states. Superpowers and weak states were thus engaged in mutual attempts to understand each other, with weak states trying to signal their commitment and superpowers trying to ascertain the trustworthiness of those signals. In short, the determination of which conflicts would be deemed relevant to the Cold War was the result of processes of interpretation and judgment rather than simply a matter of objective fact.

The Weak State's Point of View: Strategic Ideological Commitments

The division of the international community into two Cold War camps importantly structured political opportunities for leaders of weak states, as each camp promised lavish amounts of aid for deserving allies. Regardless of a leader's personal commitment to the tenets of Marxism or Western capitalism, claims of commitment to one of the ideologies could result in material benefits such as funding, weapons, military advisors, and even troops. Leaders of weak states might therefore strategically align with either ideological camp in the hopes of gaining material aid and resources from the superpowers.

These instrumental conversions were predicated on the either-or logic perpetrated by the superpowers. Regimes that criticized or opposed the United States were quickly defined as communist, encouraging that government to seek support from the Warsaw Pact. Conversely, any state that showed friendliness towards the West was regarded as anticommunist, regardless of the extent to which it substantively conformed to the Western democratic model (Graebner 2000:24; Kirkpatrick 1979). For instance, when the United States refused aid to Cuba and Nicaragua, these states began to claim stronger adherence to communist principles, in hopes of getting aid from the Soviet Union (Booth and Walker 1999; Leonard 1991). In other cases (such as Somalia), when the Soviet Union refused to fund the government, leaders turned to the United States and claimed support of Western beliefs (Lewis 1988).

The strategic nature of pseudo-ideological leanings can be seen most clearly when leaders switched beliefs. In the early 1970s, Somalia's leader Siyad Barre had declared that Somalia was henceforth dedicated to "scientific socialism" and began receiving support and military equipment from the Soviet Union (Lewis 1988:209). At that time, its neighbor Ethiopia enjoyed protection and military supplies from the United States (Lewis 1988). Then, U.S. support of Ethiopia began to wane, due in part to growing international criticism of Ethiopian human rights abuses. As U.S. aid diminished, Ethiopia began to make overtures to the Soviet Union. This new alliance between Ethiopia and the Soviet Union became problematic for Somalia, since Ethiopia and Somalia were embroiled in their own war over possession of the Ogaden, a strip of desert on the Ethiopian side of the Ethiopia-Somalia border. As the Soviets began supplying Ethiopia with military equipment, Soviet support of Somalia faded. Somalia's only choice was to turn to the other superpower, the United States and the other governments of the North Atlantic Treaty Organization, claiming to have retreated from the evils of communism. The United States responded to this about-face by providing aid and supplies to its new ally in its fight against communism (Lewis 1988).

Some scholars have similarly argued that Nicaragua's turn to communism was also an example of ideological commitments that were at least partly the result of a search for aid (Booth and Walker 1999). The solidification of the commitment of the revolutionary Nicaraguan government to communism may have been facilitated by the restrictions on military and economic aid placed by the United States and other Western countries on the new left-wing Sandinista government in 1979 (Booth and Walker 1999). Although President Carter had asked for aid in order to "maintain our ties with Nicaragua, to keep it from turning to Cuba and the Soviet Union," the U.S. Congress had restricted support, and President Reagan suspended aid entirely in 1983 (cited in Leonard 1991:175). The Soviet Union had provided only minimal assistance during the revolutionary rise to power by the Sandinistas, as the Soviets judged that the insurgency had only a small chance of success. However, once the Sandinistas gained power, the Soviet Union and Cuba responded to their requests for aid, and Nicaragua's dependence upon the communist bloc became stronger in its need to replace Western sources of aid and trade and to fight off Western-backed *contra* forces (Booth and Walker 1999). Although it is difficult to know the original beliefs of the Sandinista leaders, at least some evidence suggests that the commitment of the government to Marxist beliefs was ambiguous until it was forced to seek resources from the communist bloc (Booth and Walker 1999).

The communist side also had its share of clients run amuck. One scholar, citing the examples of Angola, Mozambique, Ethiopia, and South Yemen, commented: "many of the beneficiaries of Soviet largess have shown disturbing tendencies toward independent action when their interests diverged from those of the USSR" (MacFarlane 1990:43). For instance, Mozambique weakened its commitments to the Soviet Union and sought an agreement with the United States once the Soviet Union proved unwilling to address Mozambique's security issues with South Africa (MacFarlane 1990). As MacFarlane sums up: "In other words, although ideological affinity may be significant in influencing the initial attitudes of Marxist regimes in the third world toward the USSR, the durability of the patron client relationship appears to be, in the longer term, largely the product of material dependence" (MacFarlane 1990:43).

Again, a quote from Cold War historian John Lewis Gaddis sums up the strategic commitments of Third World allies in the Cold War:

Th[e Cold War] situation gave power to those who were supposed to have been on the receiving end of power: the "third worlders" themselves, who learned to manipulate the Americans and the Russians by laying on flattery, pledging solidarity, feigning indifference, threatening defection, or even raising the specter of their own collapse and the disastrous results that might flow from it. Like the Europeans and the Chinese, therefore, the "third world" was in a position to choose during the Cold War. (Gaddis 1997:154)

While Gaddis emphasizes that the Third World capitalized on the Cold War, the situation was really of the superpowers' own making. The superpowers saw the world through a particular lens—a historically unique set of beliefs and assumptions—that brought about this state of affairs. Thus the Western allies generally aided all states except for those whose regimes were defined as "in some measure inimical to Western interests," which meant a Marxist or pro-Soviet state (Porter 1984:218–9). Necessarily, then, those states that were not aided by the West were forced to seek aid from behind the Iron Curtain. Third World states had the power to choose, but their choices were fundamentally defined by the superpowers. And, at times, the superpowers made that choice for them.

The Superpower Point of View: Interpretation and Intervention

To some extent, leaders of weak states could manipulate the perceptions of the superpowers for their own strategic ends. At the same time, the superpowers were not passive dupes in this process, but actively interpreted and evaluated the dangers of the Cold War world for themselves. In some cases the intent of regimes and insurgents was quite clear. In other cases interpretations were based on shadowy clues and indirect evidence. Right or wrong, superpower interpretations quickly became self-fulfilling prophecies. Any action by one superpower—such as providing aid to a regime—was a clear signal that located that regime on one side of the Cold War struggle.

Interpretation was straightforward in the case of stronger, more established states. For instance, the European states declared their alliance with either the West or the Soviet bloc, and those declarations translated straight into treaty alliances, election results, and democratic or totalitarian state structures. In the Third World, however, the uncertainty of party politics made categorization difficult, and the superpowers did not always take the self-declarations of weak states at face value. Recently independent countries were usually born with fledgling state structures and lacked the fundamental infrastructure for effective governance. Given the domestic political disorder in such states, it was not surprising that they often had not clearly staked out an ideological position in the international Cold War environment. The superpowers felt such pressure to identify nascent threats, however, that they quickly sought to determine potential alliances with states whose own leaders might not have agreed upon their future ideological heading. In many cases, the superpowers developed their understanding of a conflict as pro-Western or communist out of vague hints and insubstantial clues, glued together either by potent fears or equally compelling hopes.

As a result, these processes of superpower interpretation and judgment became a self-fulfilling prophecy for the civil wars in many weak states. When one of the superpowers acted, it signaled the potential incursion of communist or pro-Western leaders and beliefs, and the state became embroiled in the Cold War whether or not that interpretation accurately reflected local perceptions. Arguably, Cuba and other Latin American countries may have become "communist problems" in large part because the United States interpreted them as communist, rather than because of their inherently communist origins. With regard to Cuba, for instance, one historian claims that "By calling Castro a Communist and acting as if he were one . . . the United States eventually contributed to his becoming a Communist and his revolution becoming anti-American" (Pastor 1987:192). In Cuba and elsewhere, the superpower interpretations disagreed with local understandings of events. Yet the interpretations of superpowers were often far more consequential than local views, because of the military aid or intervention provided by the contenders.

The U.S.-engineered civil war against Guatemalan President Jacobo Arbenz in 1954 illustrates these processes of interpretation and judgment. Scholars of the 1960s attributed the overthrow of Arbenz to capitalist interests in the banana plantations of U.S. Fruit (Schlesinger and Kinzer 1982). More recent historical work dismisses that view, instead arguing that the act was substantially motivated by fear of Soviet influence—a fear that was almost surely unfounded (Gleijeses 1991; Streeter 2000).

Jacobo Arbenz's own ideological commitments were quite ambiguous. One historian, Pietro Gleijeses, claims that in the last two years of his presidency, Arbenz considered himself a communist but decided against formally joining the Guatemalan Communist Party in the interest of public relations (Gleijeses 1991). Alternately, Gleijeses suggests that Arbenz may have had links to the CP for opportunistic reasons only, since it was the only domestic party that was likely to accept Arbenz's radical social policies (Gleijeses 1991). Richard Barnet also portrays Arbenz as using the Guatemalan Communist Party instrumentally to further his own social reforms, questioning his personal ideological commitment to communism (Barnet 1968). Even with the benefit of hindsight, therefore, Arbenz's support of communism appears ambiguous at best.

Setting aside Arbenz's personal beliefs, most historians portray his social reforms as "moderate" or as fundamentally democratic in spirit, noting that these reforms were laying "a foundation for establishing a modern, progressive state" (Gleijeses 1991:152; Streeter 2000:32). Even the Truman administration had noted that Guatemala primarily voted with the United States and the other Latin American nations on United Nations issues (Rabe 1990). In practice, therefore, Arbenz appeared indistinguishable from a liberal social reformer of a sort that would have been quite acceptable to the United States if he had come without the communist label.

At the time, however, beliefs about the Cold War world, particularly the assumption that Soviet agents were directly responsible for the spread of communism, provided a lens through which all events in Guatemala were perceived. The suspicions of the United States had been aroused by the policies implemented by Arbenz following his election in 1950. President Arbenz sought to enact a major economic transformation in Guatemala, centered on the 1952 Agrarian Reform Law that confiscated idle land and redistributed it to landless peasants (Leonard 1991; Booth and Walker 1999). This nationalization policy, in conjunction with the inclusion of known communists in the Arbenz government and suspicious events such as a weapons purchase from Czechoslovakia, caused the United States to label the Arbenz government as communist (Booth and Walker 1999).

Viewing Guatemala through the Cold War lens, U.S. officials could not imagine that communist "leanings" could be locally grown. According to the beliefs of U.S. policymakers of the time, the seed of communism must have been planted and watered by the direct interference of Soviet agents. Testifying to Congress, Senator Hickenlooper asserted that "Guatemala is in effect a Soviet [state] within Central

America, although they deny it" (cited in Streeter 2000:21). U.S. Secretary of State John Foster Dulles put this perspective even more strongly, in a speech to the tenth inter-American conference in 1954, when he "denied the existence of indigenous Communist movements and asserted that every nation in the hemisphere had been penetrated by international communism under Moscow's direction" (cited in Leonard 1991:139).

Interestingly, the United States had no direct evidence linking Guatemala with the communist leadership in the Soviet Union. John Foster Dulles told the Brazilian ambassador in 1954: "it will be impossible to produce evidence clearly tying the Guatemalan government to Moscow; that decision must be a political one and based on our deep conviction that such a tie must exist" (cited in Rabe 1990:88). Recent scholarship from the Soviet perspective also finds that Guatemala received no Soviet support in the early 1950s. In contrast to U.S. fears, the only direct contact between the Soviets and the Guatemalans had been the visit of a single Soviet diplomat attempting to purchase bananas in 1953 (Gaddis 1997; Gleijeses 1991), and Guatemala received only a single arms shipment from Czechoslovakia (Barnet 1968).

The lack of evidence, however, was not taken as a reason to question the assumption that Soviet agents had infiltrated Guatemala. Hypothetical links to Moscow, in turn, justified American plans to orchestrate a civil war to bring down Arbenz. The United States overthrew Arbenz, replacing him with a pro-American alternative. The actions of the United States, in turn, polarized the situation and actively catalyzed communist conflicts both in Guatemala and elsewhere in Latin America. Whether or not Arbenz originally had communist ideological leanings, the international interpretation of U.S. actions against Arbenz reified the Guatemalan civil war as a "communist" conflict. Communism was viewed as the prime alternative to the new U.S.-sponsored regime, and therefore became a rallying cry. In Guatemala, the U.S. intervention created widespread hostility to the new U.S.-supported Armas government, and ushered in several decades of civil war fought by communist insurgents (Streeter 2000). More generally, the intervention in Guatemala created widespread distrust throughout the region, and scholars have argued that it encouraged communist revolutionary movements in Nicaragua and El Salvador in later years (Booth and Walker 1999).

The labeling of the Arbenz government as communist by the United States resulted from a Cold War perception that allowed only two options—Arbenz was either communist or he was not. Simplistically, the United States came to see anyone who sympathized with the Soviet Union, or even proposed radical social change of any sort, as communist (Leonard 1991). The subtler notion of a politician with pro-Marxist leanings but democratic social reforms was not a possible cognitive category at that time. In Guatemala as in several other cases, the United States read "communist" influence from a variety of clues—some convincing in retrospect, others not. The ambiguous position of the Arbenz government allowed U.S. policymakers to interpret the situation in Guatemala according to their own biases.

In sum, the interpretation of ideological commitment was based upon crude indicators that were believed to signal the commitments of weak-state regimes. The most obvious indicator was a declared commitment of a government, cemented by the reciprocal granting of aid or other overtures of friendship from one or the other superpower. This might not be enough, though; the superpowers did not always take governments at their word, but looked for other indicators of their commitment such as their avowed governmental structure, voting record in the United Nations or, most damning of all, receipt of aid from the rival superpower. Complex processes of mutual understanding, or misunderstanding, could take place, therefore, as weak states tried to signal their commitment to the side that seemed instrumentally advantageous, while the superpowers tried to ascertain the true motivations behind such commitments. Superpower interpretations and self-fulfilling prophecies thus played a fundamental role in building the Cold War. Moreover, the imposition of Cold War interpretations upon ambiguous local situations and the resulting superpower actions often proved highly consequential for those civil wars labeled as Cold War conflicts.

Communist Conflicts in the Philippines

The processes of Cold War interpretation and judgment are also illustrated in the communist insurgencies in the Philippines. Accounts of the early 1950s civil war in the Philippines and the second war that recurred in 1972 straightforwardly identify the conflicts as communist insurgencies. Certainly, the United States understood these insurgencies to be communist and aided the Filipino government in suppressing them. As in the case of many conflicts of the Cold War, however, the communist allegiance of the first insurgency was debatable until the United States labeled it as such, effectively rendering it part of the Cold War. The second insurgency, in contrast, drew upon the cognitive frames from the first civil war and self-consciously labeled itself as the successor in the communist struggle. However, both civil wars were importantly motivated by the flaws of the weak Filipino state that gave legitimacy to opposition demands for state reform.

Like many other allegedly communist opposition groups, the Huks, who formed the main guerrilla force in the civil war in the late 1940s and early 1950s, were ambivalent in their adherence to Marxist tenets and there is no evidence that they were supported by the Soviet Union. The Hukbalahap (Huks) had formed as an anti-Japanese resistance group during World War II and had been prominent in the conflict against the Japanese occupation. The Huks retired at the end of the war, but re-mobilized in the late 1940s in response to political repression and economic crises that occurred under the newly independent Filipino government. The Huk insurgency was triggered by the refusal of President Roxas to seat the elected Huk representatives in the legislature along with other elected members of the Democratic Assembly, on the grounds that they were communists (Kessler 1989). Despite the accusation of communism, however, the Democratic Assembly did not appear particularly Marxist at this time. Instead, one historian described it as "an amalgamation of liberals, communists, civil liberties advocates, farmers and labor leaders" (Chapman 1987:60).

At the time the United States was convinced by Roxas' portrayal of the Democratic Assembly and the Huks as communist, as the United States was particularly ready to find communists under the bed in the early postwar years. At the time, the United States was already involved with the communist insurgency in Greece and concerned with Cold War specters in Europe. Additionally, as the recently departed imperial power from the Philippines, the United States felt a strong responsibility to ensure that the islands remained free of communist influence. It was easy for the Filipino government to convince the United States that the Huks were a communist group which naive peasants had been forced to join, a portrayal that fit well with the American tendency to see all local communist groups as controlled by Moscow. "So ironclad is [the Communists'] grip and so feared is their power . . . that the peasants dare not oppose them," reported Major Edward Lansdale, a U.S. advisor of military intelligence (cited in Shafer 1988:211). The United States had already displayed its lack of understanding of Filipino politics by backing presidential candidate Manuel Roxas, who had been a prominent politician during the Japanese occupation. General MacArthur's earnest assurance that Roxas was an innocent collaborator during the Japanese occupation had merely increased Filipino suspicion of the U.S.-endorsed government (Shafer 1988).

The local perceptions of the Huks and the extent to which they were communist were complicated and ambiguous. The Philippine Communist Party (PKP) was composed of urban intellectuals seeking revolutionary economic change on a nation-wide scale, while the Huks were primarily a peasant group, based in central Luzon, who focused on an improvement of repressive political conditions, an equitable economic situation, and participation in the political system (Shafer 1988). The Philippine Communist Party refrained from endorsing the Huk rebellion for two years after the civil war had started, as the CP did not support armed revolution (Chapman 1987). Additionally, many Huk commanders did not belong to the Philippine Communist Party and neither did the "overwhelming majority of the rank and file," a situation leading to incidents in which the Huk commanders rejected the orders of the Party leaders (Shafer 1988:233). This lack of connection between the rural Huks and the urban Communist Party leaders suggests that the Huks were not primarily a communist group, although a few of the Huk leaders were Communist Party members. In the dichotomous world of the Cold War, however, any linkage with communism was viewed at best as suspicious and at worst as damning.

The resolution of the Philippines' first civil war resulted as much (or more so) from strengthening the newly independent state as by defeating the Huks on the battleground. By the early 1950s the Huks were considered a "formidable opponent," given the limited military capabilities of the new state (Shafer 1988:213). However, the virtuoso maneuvers of Ramon Magsaysay, the newly appointed Philippine Minister of Defense, won the day. In part, Magsaysay's military tactics were a great improvement over the ineffectual sweeps of his predecessors, typical of weak state militaries. Perhaps more importantly, Magsaysay's policies reduced the maltreatment of civilians, which had been commonplace under his predecessors and which had contributed to popular support for the Huks (McDonald 1992). Another of Magsaysay's strategies, characterized as the carrot and the stick approach, led to the defection of hundreds of Huks. With one hand, Magsaysay offered lucrative rewards for turning in Huk leaders; with the other hand, signed a generous amnesty policy for former guerrillas that included the provision of farmland (MacDonald 1992).

More importantly, Magsaysay led reforms that cracked down on corruption and many of the abuses commonly perpetrated by the army, and brought greater fairness and order to the Philippines. For instance, he created a special telegraph line for any citizen to report wrongdoing by the military—resulting in a flood of complaints (Joes 2000). Moreover, his administration made significant strides in improving the fairness of the next election, which resulted in the opposition party winning every senate seat up for election (Joes 2000). This evidence that political change could be wrought without violence did much to reduce the popular support for the Huk rebellion.

The United States also played an important role behind the scenes in Magsaysay's reforms, led by U.S. Major Edward Lansdale, who was one of Magsaysay's key advisors. The director of the U.S. State Department's Philippine branch, John Melby, was also a supporter of Magsaysay's reforms. Melby agreed that the Huk revolt was due to "governmental weakness rather than Huk strength" and produced a plan for $750 million in U.S. aid to strengthen the state (Cullather 1994). With support from the United States, the first Communist insurgency in the Philippines was concluded by 1954, to the satisfaction of both the Huks and the government, in large part due to measures that strengthened the weak governmental structures and practices of the newly independent state (Arnold 1995).

By 1969 the communists were fighting again, this time against the regime of President Ferdinand Marcos. The original Huk movement in the 1940s had been a response to the corruption, abuses, and ineffectiveness of the newly independent weak Filipino state. Magsaysay had put an end to that civil war by demonstrating that government in the Philippines could be orderly and democratic, although the state remained fairly weak. By the 1970s, however, the Marcos government again displayed the weaknesses and corruption of the early Filipino

state. The army, which had shaped up under Magsaysay, had again become "rotten to the core" and rampantly corrupt (Kessler 1989:140).
This deterioration of the government was often attributed to the personal flaws of Marcos himself. As one historian sums up: "[Marcos] was
corrupt; he dismantled the democratic structures Americans prided
themselves in having bequeathed the country; he ran a venal government and an abusive military and his tenure reduced an already poor
country to near insolvency" (Chapman 1987:24). From a structural
perspective, however, the corrupt Marcos regime was quite typical of
weak states and its abuses need not be attributed to the personal flaws
of the president. Instead, it is Magsaysay's regime of democratic order-
liness and probity that appears to be a temporary exception among recently independent states of the late twentieth century.

A handful of Huks surviving from the previous war formed the nucleus of the new communist army, the NPA (New People's Army). By
the mid-1980s the NPA could claim to be operating in two-thirds of
the provinces in the Philippines (Arnold 1995). Popular support for the
NPA increased in response to the corruption, arbitrary arrests, and dis-
appearances that were prevalent under Marcos and that typify weak
state regimes generally (Brogan 1998). The NPA earned such popular
support that the U.S. Defense Department estimated that by the end of
the 1990s the NPA could have achieved parity with the security forces
of the Philippines (Arnold 1995), and one historian could confidently
state in 1989 that the Philippines Communist Party and its armed
forces "were far from beaten and in fact [remain] a formidable long-
term challenge to the government" (Jones 1989:8).

By the early 1990s the effectiveness of the NPA had dwindled. In
part, the policies of Corazón Aquino, as well as her huge popularity,
have been credited with the ebbing of the communist guerrilla insurgency. Historians and scholars of the Philippines have favored this in-
dividualistic interpretation, in which the end of both communist civil
wars was attributed to a Great Man and Woman. However, one must
also note that the waning of the communist civil war in the Philippines
coincided with the resolution of communist civil wars all around the
world. The end of the Cold War and the de-legitimation of communism as a political ideology surely played a role in the ending of the
civil war in the Philippines, although this simultaneity is surprisingly
omitted from many accounts. The unexpected termination of commu-

nist civil wars in the 1990s, many of which had already lasted many years and appeared robust in 1989, suggests that the influence of the global Cold War had important cognitive influences that have often been ignored by students of these wars.

The Cold War and Lengthy Civil Wars

The cognitive frames and material resources of the Cold War had a substantial effect on the duration of many civil wars. Communist civil wars in the post-1945 period were often quite long, averaging nearly seven years in length (for details on the coding of these wars see the Appendix). Not mere domestic disputes, these civil wars frequently drew third-party states, and sometimes the superpowers themselves, into conflicts. The Cold War provided cognitive frames and ideologies that strongly motivated participants and thereby prolonged the conflicts. Furthermore, superpowers and other interstate actors provided resources and material interventions to maintain those civil wars. Of course, both the legitimation and the resources vanished in 1989 with the end of the Cold War. As a consequence, communist civil wars throughout the world were resolved within a few years of the ending of the Cold War itself.

The Cold War's alternate visions of the state aroused passionate ideological commitments among combatants, both domestically and internationally. The availability of two alternative models played an essential role in fostering the civil conflicts of the Cold War, imbuing these conflicts with a particular intensity analogous to the religious wars of earlier centuries. For instance, the Shining Path revolt in Peru that began in the early 1980s sprang primarily from the ideological commitment of its leader to redress the poverty of the peasants and indigenous peoples. The leader of the Shining Path, Abimael Guzmán, had lived in China during the Cultural Revolution and was an adherent to the principles of Maoism (Brogan 1998). Guzmán formed the nucleus of a communist movement in a university in rural Ayacucho, where he was a professor of philosophy. Fed by a shared ideological vision, adherents to the Shining Path fought to make the hope of a communist state into a reality in Peru. The Shining Path was one of the few communist movements that did not receive aid from the Soviet Union, China, or other communist countries, relying instead on resources from its occupation of the coca-growing regions in Peru (Arnold 1991). Like other communist-inspired insurgencies around the world, however, the movement ebbed with the end of the Cold War, and had ended by 1995. With the demise of the Soviet bloc, the legitimacy and plausibility of communism as a model of governance was called into question—and social movements depending on that legitimacy collapsed.

The lengthiness of Cold War civil wars also derived from the intervention and material resources made available by superpowers. Intervention, in the form of aid, supply bases, or military troops, often proves critical for prolonging civil wars (see Chapter 6). Impoverished Third World states typically lack the domestic resources to carry on a lengthy civil war. Supplies for these conflicts must therefore come from more powerful neighbors or, in the case of the Cold War, from ideological allies. Once identified as a Cold War conflict by one of the superpowers, conflicts tended to polarize, as discussed above. Resources quickly flowed from superpowers to both the state and to the insurgents. Aided on both sides, Cold War civil wars could, and at times did, last for decades. Together, the combination of cognitive and material resources set the stage for some of the lengthiest civil wars of the period.

The effects of Cold War cognitive and material resources are powerfully illustrated by the abrupt conclusion of the civil wars following the end of the Cold War. It may, in hindsight, seem unsurprising that the end of the Cold War would have led to the end of nearly all the large-scale communist insurgencies in the world. This was not at all apparent in the early 1990s. Observers at the time were skeptical that civil wars would conclude simply because the Soviet Union had collapsed. Many of these insurgencies were not being directly maintained by Moscow, and most were not dependent upon critical supplies from the Warsaw Pact countries either; the Soviet Union had cut down its commitments to Cuba and Nicaragua by 1990 (Leonard 1991:193). Thus there seemed no necessary reason that these insurgencies would end. One scholar pointed to the communist insurgencies in the Philippines, Peru, Central America, and Cambodia that persisted until 1992 and commented:

> While the American-Soviet competition may well be ending in
> the form we have known it, it is too early to conclude confidently

that the competition between two different ideas about political and economic development—ideas that lie at the root of American and Soviet differences in the Third World—will also end. The Marxist-Leninist model can easily find new proponents even if the Soviet Union casts it off . . . Any way we view the future of Third World political development, it seems probable that the United States will find Marxist-Leninist competitors for the next five or ten years, if not far longer. (Odom 1992:54)

Another scholar commented in 1991 on the lengthy communist civil war in El Salvador that had persisted since 1979:

At the beginning of the 1990s there seemed every likelihood that the war would continue indefinitely; one American estimate suggested that on existing performance . . . it would continue to the end of the century. Eleven years of terrible brutality had polarized the two sides—the far right and extreme left—so that there seemed little prospect of either an early or an enduring settlement being reached. (Arnold 1991:545)

Shortly after the above statement was penned, however, the El Salvadoran guerrillas reached an agreement with the government, and a formal peace treaty was signed on January 15, 1992. Similarly, in Guatemala, one scholar reported in 1992 that: "The [Guatemalan] government is unlikely to destroy [the Marxist opposition forces] completely, however, and in the worst of circumstances small guerrilla cadres would probably survive in the mountains" (Odom 1992:124). Contrary to these expectations, the ending of communist civil wars in Nicaragua and El Salvador, plus the newly softened post-Cold War attitude of the United States, allowed a Guatemalan peace settlement to be signed in 1996 (Booth and Walker 1999).

The resolution of the lengthy civil wars in El Salvador, Nicaragua, and Guatemala may have been due in part to reluctance on the part of the United States to continue aiding these conflicts once the Soviet Union was no longer involved (Booth and Walker 1999). In all three countries, the rebels gained significant concessions in the peace negotiations (Brogan 1998; Montgomery 1995). Even if the United States had ceded these conflicts as fruitless, in none of these three countries did the communist forces succeed in taking over the government. In El Salvador, "the [Marxist] Democratic Revolutionary Front evaporated in the late 1980s, its place taken by dozens of non-governmental organizations" (Montgomery 1995:260). In Nicaragua, although U.S. congressional leaders congratulated themselves on ending the civil war by cutting off funding to the pro-Western contras, the pro-communist Sandinista government had already been voted out of office in 1990 by the Nicaraguan electorate and replaced by the more moderate Chamorro administration (Leonard 1991). Once the communist form of the state had ceased to be legitimate as a positive alternative to the pro-Western democratic form, proponents of communism quickly abandoned their conflicts.

The near simultaneous resolution of so many seemingly intractable civil wars immediately after the end of the Cold War is no simple coincidence. Nor is it likely the result of domestic peace-making processes, which had been ongoing for years or decades. Owing to the tremendous cognitive and material sustenance provided by the Cold War environment, these wars could not be easily resolved until the Cold War itself had been ended. The recurrence of communist conflict in the Philippines, despite the decisive conclusion of the first communist civil war, similarly suggests the persistent influence of international Cold War cognitive frames. Once the communist alternative was delegitimated by the Soviet Union itself, however, the cognitive impetus to maintain the struggles died out and the material resources also dwindled.

The sudden termination of these civil wars suggests that they were substantially based upon structural factors such as the Cold War models of the state and superpower intervention, rather than on the domestic factors of poverty and oppression that have been attributed as their cause. Poverty still exists, and is likely to continue to exist, in the Central American countries of Guatemala, El Salvador, and Nicaragua, in Cambodia, the Philippines, and rural Peru. Yet the civil wars that some claimed had been fuelled by these domestic conditions have ended without clear improvement in peasant circumstances. Instead, the end of the Cold War proved the key to resolving the conflicts.

Transnational Ideologies beyond the Cold War

The end of the Cold War has seen the demise of those civil wars to which it was linked, and a worldwide shift toward democracy and capitalism to an extent that was unexpected by pundits in the early 1990s.

Subsequently, another transnational ideology has been fingered as the successor to Communism as the primary alternative to the Western state form. In particular, the rise of Islam or, more broadly, the rise of the global non-West against the West, has been spotlighted as the "next" Cold War (Huntington 1996). As Samuel Huntington ominously predicts: "Power is shifting from the long predominant West to non-Western civilizations" (Huntington 1996:29).

While it is possible that these ideologies may develop in the future into transnational ideologies that prolong civil wars, this has not yet come to pass. Drawing from the experience of the Cold War, the Islamic movement currently lacks critical components that would lead to intractable polarized civil wars, although these components may develop in the future. First, the movement lacks consensus on a common model of the state to challenge the democratic/pro-Western model. Second, Islamic states do not yet intervene on behalf of a monolithic Islamic ideology, but pursue a variety of more specific national interests. One may speculate, however, that the United States appears to be building Islam into a monolithic enemy, which may prove consequential in future years.

Potent transnational ideologies (such as communism) provide a model of the state that is a viable alternative to the currently legitimate model circulating in the international community. This model of the state must be internationally validated and given external legitimacy broadly. During the Cold War, the Western-democratic and communist models of the idealized state were both legitimate in the international community, although, of course, separately endorsed and not always followed in practice. Currently, however, an international consensus on an idealized model of the Islamic state does not appear to exist, as illustrated by the significant dissension among Islamic states in practice and in policy over the proper definition of an Islamic state. Although one-fifth of the world's population can be counted as Muslim, there is great diversity among different Islamic groups (Esposito 1999). As John Esposito (1999:228) warns: "The creation of an imagined monolithic Islam leads to a religious reductionism that views political conflicts in the Sudan, Lebanon, Bosnia, and Azerbaijan in primarily religious terms as 'Islamic-Christian conflicts.'" Instead, he points out that "local disputes and civil wars have more to do with political issues (e.g., ethnic nationalism, autonomy, and independence) and socioeconomic issues and grievances than with religion" (Esposito 1999:228).

Furthermore, the example of the Cold War suggests that transnational political and military resources, motivated by theories necessitating intervention in civil wars, form an important mechanism by which civil wars are prolonged. Like the Cold War, the conflict between Islam and the West is usually conceptualized as an interstate conflict. Islam might also become a basis for domestic civil wars in the future, in which proponents of the Islamic model of the state contend against supporters of the Western democratic model, both sides supported by interstate resources. Currently, however, broad international support for such civil wars, along the lines of the Cold War, does not yet appear to have developed. For instance, in the current Israeli-Palestinian conflict there are six main Islamic factions, each with different ties to Iran, Syria, or Libya, rather than a unified international Islamic force. Different national interests have led to different alliances, rather than a united Islamic movement against the West (Rubin 2003:210). John L. Esposito comments: "Monolithic Islam is a recurrent Western myth that has never been borne out by the reality of Muslim history" (Esposito 1999:225). As evidence, he (1999:225–226) points to intra-Islamic conflicts in which Libya's Qaddafi has been a "bitter enemy" of Islamic leaders Sadat of Egypt and Nimieri of the Sudan, while Iran has politically opposed both Saudi Arabia and Iraq.

Although neither Islam nor the global South have currently developed as transnational ideologies with the capacity for prolonging civil wars, such development is not ruled out in the future. Indeed, the United States seems to have done much recently to promote the development of a transnational Islamic ideology. Similar to its stance during the early Cold War, the United States appears to be re-conceptualizing the world as bipolar, reifying the distinction between the West and the Islamic states that may force the development of an alliance among the states of the "axis of evil." This may be hastened along by the U.S. tendency to see Islam as a monolithic movement. For instance, Speaker of the House Newt Gingrich claimed in 1995 that "There is a worldwide phenomenon of Islamic totalitarianism funded and largely directed by the state of Iran" (cited in Esposito 1999:213). The lack of a monolithic center for Islam is illustrated by the different states that have been claimed as the center, including not only Iran, but also Algeria and Iraq.

In a very real sense, the United States seems to be building its own enemy out of a set of formerly heterogeneous and divided states. Historically, the Islamic states have frequently disagreed among themselves on the proper form of the Islamic state and their shared political interests. But the powerful beliefs and interpretations of the United States, coupled with its willingness to provide intervention and military resources, may succeed in creating unity among the formerly divided Islamic states. Although perceptions are contingent rather than necessary, the consequences of those perceptions can be quite real and deadly, as the case of transnational Islam may prove.

6

Interstate Interventions in Civil Wars

CIVIL WARS ARE OFTEN complicated by the intervention of third-party states. Foreign governments that take an interest in civil conflicts may bring their own forces to bear on one side or another, or they may provide various forms of aid that significantly alter the course of a war. Prior research on intervention has principally focused on the intervening state—its strategies, motivations, and the extent to which those motivations are consistent with the strictures of international law (Hoffmann 1996; Damrosch 1993; Bull 1986; Vincent 1974; Tillema 1973; Higgins 1972). Much less attention has been paid to the effects of these interventions on the course and duration of civil wars. I discuss the increased occurrence of intervention and its effect on weak state civil wars and review the handful of empirical studies that have examined the effect of intervention on the duration of civil war. In general, these studies find that interventions have increased the length of civil wars since 1945.

One of the conundrums of intractable civil wars is: how can Third World states, many of which have difficulty feeding and housing their people, find the resources to wage civil wars for years or decades? The answer is that the resources necessary to perpetuate the conflict often come from outside the territorial borders of the state. Interstate interventions, defined broadly, have figured in most of the civil wars fought since World War II (Luard 1972). Amazingly, as many as 71 percent of

130

the civil wars that have occurred since 1945 have involved support by an external power (see Chapter 2). As one scholar notes: "Virtually all insurgencies depend to an appreciable extent on external support, most obviously for access across the border of a neighboring state which is prepared at least to turn a blind eye to its activities, but also for weapons, money, diplomatic backing and . . . even food" (Clapham 1998:15).

Intervention in the Postwar World

Interstate intervention is hardly a new phenomenon. Arguably, intervention has been a part of international politics since the beginnings of the international system (Krasner 1999). Some have even claimed that all of international politics is only intervention in various forms and degrees of politeness (Hoffman 1984). As the international system has changed after World War II, however, the type and frequency of interventions have changed correspondingly (Boli 2001). Before World War II, most interventions were carried out by the Great Powers, either in concert or unilaterally (Leurdijk 1986; Carre 1968; Phillips 1920). Great Power interventions were typically (though not exclusively) strong and decisive, involving large military forces supporting one side of a civil war, and resulting in rapid resolution of conflict. If anything, nineteenth-century interventions shortened the length of civil wars.

Interventions in the post-1945 era have become much more common than in earlier historical periods and involve countries at all levels of military capability. Interventions are carried out by former colonial powers, regional powers, and neighboring countries, in addition to the superpowers. In particular, regional powers such as China, India, Indonesia, Egypt, Libya, Turkey, Syria, Cuba, and Vietnam have figured prominently in the civil wars of the late twentieth century (Bull 1984). Another difference from the past is that milder forms of intervention, such as provision of supplies of weapons, aid, advisors, and bases, have largely supplanted the more aggressive actions. Rather than decisively resolving conflicts with large military forces, postwar intervention usually only provides sufficient resources to allow a conflict to continue.

Again, post-World War II interventions are often dual-sided. Almost half of all civil wars fought since 1945 saw external support given to both sides of the conflict (see Chapter 2 and Appendix). The effects of dual-sided intervention can greatly extend the length and intensity of a civil war by pouring resources into opposing sides, adding more and more fuel to the fire. Often one set of states intervenes by propping up a government—perhaps one so weak that it would otherwise have folded—while other states support opposition coalitions that may also be quite weak and in significant disarray. In extreme cases, such as the Chadian civil war discussed below, third parties drove the conflict more than local actors did. These dual-sided interventions have been a major factor sustaining and prolonging the civil wars of the post-World War II period.

The literature offers little examination or explanation of the changing nature of intervention in the postwar era. A variety of factors may be involved, including Cold War deterrence, the globalization of state interests, or technological advances in military transportation. The proliferation of weak states, in and of itself, increases the frequency of intervention and the participation by regional powers. The fragility of newly independent states creates a variety of forms of local or regional instability that can be a magnet for intervention. Moreover, the world polity processes that encouraged the proliferation of weak states in the first place—namely, those supporting decolonization and discouraging territorial war—unintentionally encourage intervention as an alternative. Great Powers historically achieved goals through territorial invasion or colonization, acts which have become rare since 1945. The former is less legitimate and involves substantially greater political costs than in centuries past, while the latter has become almost unthinkable. In such an international environment, indirect intervention (military aid or advisors) becomes an attractive and low-cost option.

Throughout, the term "intervention" should be taken broadly, as including both the mild and more aggressive forms of intervention. Direct military intervention, in which troops from the intervening state take part in the civil war, occurs in a small number of civil wars. Milder forms of intervention are more common, including the provision of support in the form of weapons, training, transport, military advisors, or allowing insurgents to set up bases in the intervening country. The last of these, provision of bases, is a particularly important form of intervention that often proves to be critical in shaping the course of weak state civil wars.

Intervention in Chad

Many studies begin with the presumption that civil wars are triggered and maintained by local actors in response to local issues, while they ignore or downplay the effects of third-party intervention. Consider the following description of the civil war in Chad, which, similar to many accounts, gives primacy to local actors and their interests:

> In *Chad*, northern populations who suffered neglect and repression at the hands of the southern-run, newly-independent government, broke out in rebellion in 1965, organized in various factions of the National Liberation Front of Chad (FroLiNaT) with Libyan support . . . The civilian government fell in 1978 to its own military, which in turn fell to the FroLiNaT factions in 1980. Thereafter, the conflict continued among the factions. (Zartman 1992:28)

This account implies that domestic inequalities between north and south were both the initial cause of the war and the factor that continued to motivate it. Although the writer acknowledges the support of Libya, that country is given a secondary role in this admittedly brief description of the conflict, and the account ignores entirely the military involvement of France and numerous other countries that played a critical role in supporting the government and maintaining the conflict. A more detailed historical account shows that the interventions by regional and global powers were critical factors that sustained the war in Chad for nearly a decade. The confusing course of the civil war in Chad, in which factions quickly rose, fell, and realigned, was driven by the changing alignments and realignments of the domestic factions with the various intervening states.

Accounts of the civil war in Chad often begin by pointing out the political and economic inequalities between northern and southern Chad. And yet impoverished peoples, such as the chiefly nomadic peoples of northern Chad, typically lack the resources necessary to organize a serious military effort. On a per capita income of $180 a year, it is hard to believe that the economy of Chad would support a protracted civil war (Brogan 1998). Thus it should come as little surprise that both sides required substantial aid for the conflict to escalate into a protracted civil war.

The northern insurgents were aided by Libya throughout the conflict. Libya had a clear self-interest guiding its intervention: hopes of annexing the Aouzou strip, which lay between northern Chad and Libya. Libya's territorial ambitions were arguably the primary force behind the war in Chad. The militarily powerful Libyan government could have simply marched into Chad, but such actions are highly illegitimate in the international system and would likely have provoked a strong response from the world polity. Instead, Libya gave support to insurgents who, in exchange, would concede the Aouzou strip if victorious. If not for counterintervention from other countries, Libya would probably have had its way in wresting the desired territory from the weak government of Chad. France, though, as the former colonial power of Chad, supported Chadian sovereignty—at first its incumbent southern-based government—through its strong military opposition of Libya's territorial ambitions. When a faction of northern guerrillas (not associated with Libya) ousted the southern government, France supported the new northern-based government over the Libyan-sponsored northern insurgents.

Libya and France were not the only players. Zaire, Nigeria, Togo, Senegal, Benin, Guinea, and the forces of the Organization of African Unity were all involved in the conflict at one time or another (Somerville 1990). Moreover, Algeria, Sudan, Egypt, Cameroon, and other African countries played supporting roles. For instance, Habre and Goukouni—two northern opposition leaders—fled to Cameroon in alternate periods when their fortunes were ebbing. The superpowers had their fingers in this pie as well. The Soviet Union was accused of placing advisors in Libya, while the United States sent planes and missiles to aid one of the northern leaders after he became the new president of Chad (Somerville 1990; Brogan 1998).

The conflict had its origins in the grievances held by northerners against the south. But it is unlikely that the conflict could have escalated militarily without external support. Once Libya began to provide military and financial support for the northern rebels, the guerrillas began to have a much greater military impact, escalating a minor rebellion in the periphery into a full-scale civil war. Indeed, the northern troops were so successful that one of their leaders, Hissene Habre, ousted the southern president and was installed as the new president of Chad in 1980.

If the conflict were truly local in origin, one would have expected that the establishment of a government composed of northerners would mitigate the original grievances of the northern population of Chad and produce a lasting peace. In reality, it was at that point that the war accelerated in terms of scope and casualties, when the northern-based government began fighting another faction of northern insurgents. The critical distinction between the northern factions was not based on ethnicity, religion, or ancient grievances, but on their positions towards Libya's territorial ambitions. The northern leader who was the new head of the government, Hissene Habre, was opposed to Libya's territorial claims, while another northern leader, Goukouni, supported Libya's claims. The international pressures generated by Libya encouraged the continuation of the war, with Libya supporting Goukouni and the ex-colonial power, France, supporting the government of Habre. With substantial international involvement on both sides, the two groups of northerners (the government and the opposition) continued to fight each other, with both sides occasionally fighting groups of southerners who were no longer in control of the government. Indeed, the war continued even after Goukouni attempted to make peace with Habre.

Eventually, Goukouni's northern troops joined together with Habre's northern troops (Brogan 1998). Even this reunification of the northern leaders did not end the war. The civil war continued, with Goukouni's and Habre's troops alike fighting against Libyan troops and mercenaries from Sudan and Lebanon (Brogan 1998). At this point, the war had essentially ceased to be a civil war, with most of the Chadian factions aligned together against Libya. In time Libya agreed to withdraw and the "civil" war in Chad ended. These confusing political realignments make no sense if one takes seriously the claim that the war was rooted fundamentally in northern/southern grievances. The events of the war come into focus only after one realizes that Libya, France, and other countries were essentially having their own war in which Chad provided the playing board.

The naive story of northern oppression of the south gives way to a far more complex picture. In a sense, the civil war in Chad could be considered a tool of interstate rivalry and intervention. Much of the impetus for the war can be laid at the door of the various intervening states. Although the origins of the conflict lay in initial grievances of the north against the south, and thousands of Chadians certainly fought and died in the civil war (perhaps 50,000 casualties total since 1965, according to Arnold 1991), the civil war in impoverished Chad could not have been sustained without the substantial resources and military involvement provided by external actors. Sadly, such intervention is now so common as to be routine. Chad is but one of many cases in which a post-1945 civil war has been lengthened through intervention by third parties.

Interventions in Weak States

Weak state civil wars are magnets for third-party intervention. The dominant image of interventions is that of Great Power and superpower intervention in which powerful external actors take sides in a civil conflict (or even instigate one) to ensure that a friendly regime is in place. In addition, several other scenarios, not discussed in the intervention literature, have become increasingly common in the post-1945 world. First, interventions are often used as a general-purpose means of prosecuting interstate conflict. Because the world polity frowns upon direct territorial aggression, indirect acts such as intervention have become a common and low-cost way of pursuing interstate rivalry. Other interventions arise out of efforts to bolster the sovereignty of weak states. Governments threatened by civil war often request help from a former colonial power or the international community in an effort to shore up their lack of military capability. In another variant, states often intervene in the affairs of weaker neighbors to control their own domestic insurgencies.

Great Power Interventions to Choose Regimes

The classic notion of intervention involves external powers working to preserve or install a favorable regime. The United States routinely supported pro-U.S. regimes that were threatened by communist insurgents, and also pro-capitalist insurgents that sought to supplant communist regimes. (Similarly, during the nineteenth century, the Great Powers often intervened to quash incipient democratic movements or revolutions in support of monarchical regimes.) Such interventions usually resulted in a quick resolution to civil wars, unless powerful nations propped up both sides of a civil conflict, as was the case in several Cold War interventions. This sort of intervention has been much discussed in the literature (and in Chapter 5) and warrants little further treatment, other than to note that many post-1945 interventions do not fit this model.

Intervention as Interstate Conflict

The proliferation of weak states and corresponding changes in the international community have led to the use of intervention as a means of pursuing interstate rivalry or aggression. In previous historical eras, interstate territorial aggression was a routine method of combating interstate rivals. Since the end of World War II, however, international norms and laws proscribing territorial invasion have become increasingly institutionalized in the world polity, accompanied by a substantial decline in territorial war (Zacher 2001; Hironaka 1998). Whereas territorial aggression often prompts strong international rebuke and expends a great deal of diplomatic capital, interventions—especially the milder forms such as the provision of arms to insurgents—are scarcely noticed by the international community. For instance, had Libya used its own troops to annex territory from Chad, rather than supporting pro-Libyan insurgents, there is little doubt that significant international rebuke would have followed. This international environment provides strong incentives for states to pursue the strategy of intervention. Moreover, the proliferation of weak states makes intervention an attractive option. Interventions against strong states are less effective and more dangerous: teasing a lion might lead to strong retaliation. One need only note the care with which the United States and the Soviet Union played their games of brinksmanship to recognize the difficulties of intervening in the concerns of a strong state. In a world of weak states, however, even modest interventions can have powerful effects—and fewer dangers—making it a useful strategy for the pursuit of interstate conflict.

Consequently, states have opted to use intervention instead of (or more rarely, in addition to) territorial aggression as a means of pursuing contested territory. This tactic was illustrated in the case of Chad, where Libya clearly hoped that intervention in support of the northern rebels would provide the means of gaining territory in the Aouzou strip (Brogan 1998). Even if the intervention does not directly involve direct territorial gain, it can provide a means for carrying out an interstate rivalry that may have developed over territorial disputes. India, for example, intervened on behalf of East Pakistan (now Bangladesh) during its war of secession from Pakistan in 1971, in large part because of India's ongoing dispute with Pakistan over the border between them (Arnold 1991). Ethiopia and Somalia have each supported insurgents in the other country as a means to gaining control over the contested Ogaden territory that lies between them (Arnold 1991; Regan 2000). These forms of intervention have been fairly moderate, harassing the rival state but insufficient to overthrow or severely undermine its government.

Interventions in Support of Weak State Sovereignty

With the proliferation of weak states comes the perpetual threat of collapsing regimes. Increasingly, interventions are mounted to protect the continued existence and functioning of weak Third World states. These weak states may have little or no geopolitical significance. Whether driven by humanitarian concerns, alliance commitments, or other interests, third parties often work to buttress the sovereignty and stability of Third World states experiencing civil war—usually at the direct request of the regime. Such interventions commonly involve the extension of significant external aid or direct military assistance for combating opposition groups.

Former colonial powers, such as Britain and France, have frequently intervened in their ex-colonies at the request of the beleaguered governments. The ex-colonial powers have tended to accept responsibility to help their former colonies maintain their statehood and some degree of social order. Thus the French intervention in the former French colony of Chad, at the request of the Chadian government, falls into this category. One scholar estimates that France has intervened at least twenty times in former French territories (Somerville 1990). In addition, many of the former French colonies in Africa have military or defense agreements with France providing weapons, training, advisors, and French military bases. Although Britain has intervened somewhat less actively than France has, it also has provided arms, training, and advisors for several of its former colonies (Somerville 1990). Again, this is not to say that there is no self-interest operating—the French intervention in Chad, for instance, was arguably motivated by French interests in the development of stronger ties with sub-Saharan French-speaking African countries (Somerville 1990). However, the result of these interventions has frequently been the support of the incumbent governments of recently independent weak states.

In addition to states, international entities such as the United Nations or the Organization of African Unity have intervened on behalf of national sovereignty. Since 1945, the United Nations has increasingly found itself involved in civil wars as an observer, provider of humanitarian aid or assistance, and more rarely, peacekeeper (United Nations 1990). But given that the mandate for the United Nations peacekeeping forces is to enforce regional security rather than resolve national problems, they are not necessarily a factor promoting the resolution of a civil war (MacQueen 1999). Scholars have found that United Nations interventions have apparently had "no effect on the occurrence, timing, or severity of future conflicts" as illustrated by several cases in which civil wars have recurred following a peacekeeping mission (Diehl, Reifschneider and Hensel 1996:697). More optimistic observers hope, as one claims, "though the UN missions did not immediately bring the wars concerned to an end, there is scarcely a single one in which the situation was not improved through their operations" (Luard 1972:216). The United Nations' interventions may have reduced the intensity of fighting in some cases, but they do not appear to have had a general effect on the shortening of civil wars or in preventing their recurrence.

Finally, international development aid, while not considered intervention per se, has also served to significantly bolster the sovereignty of weak states. Despite its significance, scholars have generally failed to examine the effects of development aid on civil wars (with the welcome exception of Esman and Herring 2001). This support includes nonmilitary aid, in the form of the normal workings of the international development regime such as development aid and loans. Most commonly, aid comes from international organizations such as the World Bank and the United Nations, and bilateral sources among the Western industrialized states or the Warsaw Pact. Although not formally intended for military purposes, foreign aid is nearly always channeled through the state and may be diverted to sustain an ongoing war. Even when used for its intended purposes, aid typically supports the government, builds economic infrastructure, and otherwise bolsters the incumbent regime. Although development aid is not usually discussed as a type of intervention—and is not included in the definition of intervention used in this chapter—it provides an important and overlooked source of support for the state engaged in civil war. It is important to recall that the world polity provides general support for weak states that contributes to the maintenance of the façade of statehood, and by implication shores up the central government that is the official authority in that state.

Ex-colonial powers, international forces, and others typically intervene to prevent the collapse of the existing government. Their efforts do not necessarily shorten the civil war, especially in cases where a weak government would otherwise have been decisively defeated by opposition forces. Yet these interventions have an important consequence, drastically reducing the number of states that utterly collapse as the result of civil conflict.

Interventions to Control Domestic/Regional Conflicts

States may intervene in other states as part of efforts to pursue their own domestic insurgents, who hide within the borders of a neighboring weak state or otherwise garner support from a weak state. These insurgent tactics result from the inability of weak states to control their own borders, providing an opportunity for insurgents or refugees to spill across into the weak state. To root out their own insurgents, neighbors often end up intervening in the weak state—either to bolster the regime sufficiently to enable the border to be closed, or to replace the regime with one willing to crack down on the insurgents of its neighbor. The weak state may or may not intend to abet their neighbor's insurgents. Weak states may be too wrapped up in their own civil war to enforce border crossings, or they may do nothing in order to show their sympathies towards the rebels.

The Rhodesian and South African intervention in Mozambique is an extreme example of such an intervention. In the 1970s, the white governments of Rhodesia and South Africa were threatened by growing domestic insurgencies, which had set up bases in neighboring Angola and Mozambique. Rhodesia and South Africa feared that the all-black governments in southern Africa would support their anti-apartheid insurgents and would ultimately threaten their domestic polities. As a means of controlling their own rebel groups, therefore, Rhodesia and South Africa supported antigovernment insurgents in both Angola and Mozambique. The main insurgent group in Mozambique, RENAMO, was built virtually from scratch by Rhodesia when Mozambique became independent in 1975 (Arnold 1991; Vines 1991). When the all-white government in Rhodesia fell in 1980 and became the government of Zimbabwe, South Africa continued to maintain support for RENAMO. South Africa was particularly motivated to continue its intervention because Mozambique was providing bases for South Africa's own insurgents in its apartheid civil war by this time (Hall and Young 1997). As the political climate in southern Africa changed in the 1990s, however, South Africa withdrew its support. The civil war in Mozambique, which had essentially been created by interstate intervention, faded away after the withdrawal of external support (Brogan 1998).

Regional conflicts can spill into weak states in a similar manner. For instance, Palestinian insurgents and refugees from the Arab-Israeli conflicts fled across the Israeli border into Lebanon following the wars of the 1960s and 1970s. In 1978, Israel intervened in the ongoing Lebanese civil war in an attempt to control Palestinian insurgents who were disrupting internal politics in Israel from territorial bases in Lebanon (Brogan 1998). Israel continued to supply arms to Lebanese Christians who were engaged in the Lebanese civil war even after Israel's military withdrawal, following the installation of a UN peacekeeping force (Arnold 1991). Israel invaded Lebanon a second time in 1982, again in an attempt to destroy bases of the Palestinian Liberation Organization, leading to massive damage to Beirut and southern Lebanon (Arnold 1991). Israel's interests in controlling its own domestic conflicts strongly motivated these interventions, but the prerequisite was the weakness of the Lebanese state. Lebanon failed to prevent the settlement of Palestinians in the first place, and was unable (and perhaps unwilling) to prevent armed Palestinian forays into Israel.

Interventions of this sort have typically been perpetrated by militarily strong neighbors or regional powers, rather than by world superpowers or the European states. These neighboring states are engaged in domestic or interstate conflicts of their own, in which their weaker neighbors are actively aiding or passively abetting insurgents. Prevented by international laws from outright territorial annexation, the regional powers resort to intervention in retaliation—actively aiding insurgents based in the territory of their weaker neighbor—as a means of controlling their own conflicts.

Effects of Intervention

Strong states have large internal resources, so only very substantial interventions are likely to sway the outcome of a civil war in such circumstances. In weak states, by contrast, the resources provided by intervening parties are highly consequential. Many post-1945 civil wars cannot be thought of as merely being aided by interstate interventions, but instead are fundamentally sustained by them. The resources provided by intervening states may exceed, often substantially, the amount of resources available within the country in which the civil war is being fought. For instance, when India intervened in the Sri Lankan civil war, the size of the Indian contingent was larger than the size of the entire Sri Lankan army (Tillema 1991).

The impact of intervention depends on the particular circumstances. I suggest two ideal-typical extremes, which delineate the range of common outcomes. The first ideal type is a decisive one-sided intervention that produces an immediate resolution to civil conflict. Many nineteenth-century Great Power interventions and some Cold War interventions fit this type (Carre 1968; Phillips 1920). When overwhelming force is marshaled on one side of a conflict, wars end rapidly. The opposing side is either quickly defeated or gives up without a fight, facing insurmountable odds.

The brief civil war in Costa Rica in 1948 provides an example of how decisive intervention can shorten a conflict. In this civil war, domestic opposition forces revolted in protest of the fraudulent election practices that had led to the installation of Rafael Calderón Guardia as president. The opposition received clandestine aid from Nicaragua and Honduras, which provided bases and manpower to the anti-Guardia rebels. The addition of Nicaraguan and Honduran resources to those already commanded by the opposition forces gave them enough power to overcome the government forces, although it is possible that the opposition would have been successful even without intervention. As a result, the civil war lasted only a few months and the leader of the opposition, José Figueres Ferrer, quickly assumed the presidency (Booth and Walker 1999; Tillema 1991; Arnold 1991).

Most post-1945 civil wars follow a rather different trajectory. A second ideal type involves multiple intervening parties and significant resources flowing to both sides of a civil conflict. Or, alternately, a well-organized and resource-rich state may be fighting an exogenously supported insurgency. Let us call this situation a war with infinite resources. Obviously, this is an exaggeration, since even the most wealthy and supportive of allies will eventually reach their limit and reduce supplies or withdraw from the conflict. Compared to the domestic resources available to combatants in a weak state, however, the resources supplied by third parties can be huge. For instance, British journalist Anthony Sampson has described the Middle East as a seemingly endless arms race in which the major powers have "poured in arms on both sides in a succession of balances and counterbalances" (cited in Hartung 1994:198). With British understatement, he notes that this has made arms control in the region more difficult.

What is the effect of dual-sided intervention and infinite resources on civil wars? Civil conflicts typically escalate. External arms and resources result in more ferocious conflicts and much higher casualties than would otherwise be the case (Regan 2000; Jentleson, Levite and Berman 1992). As happened in Chad, as many as ten or more external parties might contribute to a civil conflict, providing arms, bases, military advisors, and resources to various factions, with correspondingly high casualties.

Wars of infinite resources tend to persist. With a continuous stream of resources, both sides can continue fighting indefinitely. Consider the civil war in Sri Lanka, which has lasted over twenty years. The war has been perpetuated by the nearly infinite supply of money and arms available to the opposition group. Not only did the Tamil Tigers received support from external states, but they have also been supported by wealthy Tamil expatriates living in Canada, Britain, Switzerland, and Australia, who reportedly contribute $1 million a month (Smith 1999). One of the best-supplied rebel groups in the world, the Tamil Tigers have developed an extensive arms trade network that extends to Hong Kong, Singapore, Lebanon, Cyprus, Thailand, Burma, Ukraine,

Bulgaria, and North Korea (cited in Sislin and Pearson 2001). Steeped in resources, the Tamils are virtually unique in the world of guerrilla insurgencies in that they own a fleet of five or six freighters to transport weapons they have purchased in the world's black market (Smith 1999). The Tamil Tigers reportedly also have their own munitions factory that produces mortars, grenades, and land mines. Sislin and Pearson (2001:89) summarize: "few ethnic groups in other states have had such a well-developed supply system."

The repeated failure of negotiations in Sri Lanka may be attributed to the situation of the Tamil Tigers, whose forces are so well funded that they have no need to negotiate or attempt to end the civil war. At least 50,000 people have been killed in the Sri Lankan civil war since 1983, while hundreds of thousands more are homeless or refugees, and the end of the war is not yet in sight (Brogan 1998). As one scholar notes, Sri Lanka poses "a peculiar case, where peace may never be achieved . . . unless the conditions for continuous reproduction of war are effectively managed" (Uyangoda 1999:158). While the Tamils represent an extreme case, the general process of infinite resources obtains in many civil wars. Similar difficulties of negotiation in Northern Ireland and Palestine may also have resulted from the large amounts of resources available to both the state and the opposition in these conflicts.

Given the condition of infinite resources fueling the conflict on both sides and the proposition that fighting will continue as long as sufficient resources are obtainable, the ensuing civil war could be lengthy indeed. Indeed, the conflict might not be ended until intervention is withdrawn on one or both sides, as in the case of Mozambique and Chad. These conditions could incur enormous costs to both parties in a war, greatly outweighing any possible benefits. Even if one side eventually obtained victory, the costs might be so high that no victory could be worth it from a cost/benefit point of view. For instance, North Vietnam won its war against South Vietnam, but the costs were so high that even fifteen years later it could be claimed as an economic backwater and one of the least developed countries in the world (Ikle 1991). Similarly, Uganda, one of the most promising and prosperous of the British colonies of Africa, became an economic catastrophe after decades of civil war. Mozambique also suffered as a result of its civil war, and was listed as the unhappiest country on earth in the *International Index of Human Suffering* in 1992 (Brogan 1998).

How well does the model of infinite resources apply to actual cases of civil wars? The wars in Chad and Mozambique, discussed earlier in this chapter, were clearly massively supported through intervention, and in the case of Mozambique the civil war was even started by intervening third-party states. Empirical studies suggest that the greater the intervention (in terms of numbers of intervening states), the lengthier the civil war. For instance, Regan (2000) has examined 138 civil conflicts from 1945 to 1994 (his list uses a cutoff figure of 200 casualties rather than 1,000). Of the 49 conflicts that did not experience third-party intervention, the average length that had ended by 1994 was only 1.5 years. In contrast, of the 89 conflicts that did experience intervention, the average length was substantially greater—those that had ended by 1994 averaged 7 years in length. Regan also shows that the more countries that intervene in a war, the longer the duration of the war tended to be. Similarly, studies by Elbadawi and Sambanis (2000), Small and Singer (1982), and Pearson (1974) have also shown that "internationalized" civil wars have much greater casualties and that interventions increase levels of violence and exacerbate instability. Although intervention is not the end of the story of protracted civil war—in Regan's study, of the 18 wars without intervention that were ongoing in 1994 the mean duration was quite lengthy, nearly 18 years—clearly, interstate intervention is an important factor in the explanation of intractable civil wars (Regan 2000).

Thus interventions may encourage civil wars to escalate by providing the resources necessary for initial mobilization, resulting in wars that do not end until the intervening state withdraws. With near-infinite resources, combatants might not be motivated to take negotiations seriously, since they have the resources to continue the conflict. Governments can thus pour the resources of an entire country into the conflict, and even be aided by another country, and still not be able to control rebel groups aided by outsiders. Intervention may cause civil wars to drag on for years or decades, with no end in sight.

Perils of Intervention for the Intervening State

Not only does the target state suffer the effects of intervention; the intervening state does too. While scholars have studied in detail whether interventions were legitimate according to international law (Hoffman

1996; Damrosch 1993; Bull 1986; Vincent 1974; Tillema 1973; Higgins 1972; Brownlie 1963), less attention has been paid to whether the outcome of those interventions turned out as the policymakers originally hoped. I suggest that intervention in civil wars frequently results in undesirable outcomes for the intervening state in the long term, because policymakers failed to take into consideration the fundamental weaknesses of the state that is the target of the intervention.

At first glance, it might seem reasonable for a state to intervene in an ongoing civil war in order to install a regime that would be favorable to its interests or to oppose the intervention of a third state. This option seems inexpensive, as intervention frequently does not cost in lives for the intervening state but merely in resources. But subsequent costs may result from the failure of the intervening state to appreciate the fundamental weaknesses of the government and opposition coalitions. Hence the intervening state may find itself in the unhappy position of supporting a weak state for decades against subsequent rebellions, even after the "successful" termination of the civil war. In addition, if the regime it has supported is overthrown, the intervening state may find itself cast as the enemy of the successive regime, leading to a long-term loss of influence and the potential for alliance with that state.

One common outcome is that the intervening state ends up propping up a weak and increasingly corrupt state when the intervention is successful. In an intervention in a strong state, the intervening state could rely on the newly installed regime to remember the favor without further support once the civil war had concluded to its satisfaction. There intervention offers the benefits of having a friendly regime in power, while expending only the normal costs of the civil war intervention. In an intervention in a weak state, however, the new regime is often unable to stand on its own even after the civil war is over. In order to protect its investment, the intervening state may feel compelled to buttress the new regime, at a cost of millions or billions of dollars more than its initial investment in the civil war.

Additionally, intervention on one side of a civil war frequently leads to the construction of the intervening state as an enemy to the opposing side of the war, with possible long-term costs. In a strong state this possibility might not be of great concern to the intervening state. As long as the side it supports emerges victorious, the opinions of the defeated party are of little importance. In weak states, however, the likelihood is high that the regime supported by the intervention will eventually be overthrown, despite an initial victory. The instability of these governments is fundamentally due to the structural weaknesses of the state, rather than the stances of leaders. Thus the new regime is likely to turn to the corruption, discriminatory policies, and human rights abuses that it denounced in its predecessor, in an effort to prevent its own downfall. These repressive policies, in turn, provide the rationale for new domestic challengers that arise to take advantage of the opportunities of state weakness. The intervening state may find itself in the unenviable position of supporting a corrupt and tottering regime against new insurgencies. The instability and quick turnover in governments evident in weak states creates the likelihood that intervention in a civil war, even if initially successful for the intervening state, will create an enemy that will compromise future interests of the intervening state. Thus long-term interests may be harmed, despite the short-term benefits for the intervening state.

For instance, the United States was able to install Mohammed Reza Pahlavi as the Shah of Iran in 1953 as the result of a coup generally attributed to the Central Intelligence Agency, which overthrew the democratically elected Iranian leader Mossadegh. For over two decades this was heralded as one of the successes of U.S. foreign policy. The United States was pleased to have a friendly government in power even though the new Iranian regime was not strong enough to support itself, relying upon the United States for aid and advanced weaponry (Hartung 1994). Despite this assistance, however, Iran still suffered from structural weaknesses. These weaknesses prompted repressive policies as a way for the government to maintain its power. In turn, these "repressive policies, rampant corruption in [the Shah's] inner circle, and vast inequalities of wealth and income" fueled a revolutionary movement that successfully overthrew the Shah in 1978 (Hartung 1994:82). Moreover, the support that the United States had given the unpopular leader made it a central target of the revolutionary movement. The new leader, Ayatollah Khomeini, rose to power on strong anti-American sentiments that were expressed in the short term by the taking of hostages from the U.S. embassy in Iran and in a long-term opposition to the United States.

Despite the short-term success of its installation of the Shah, the United States eventually suffered from its intervention. First, the

United States poured large amounts of resources into Iran in order to maintain the increasingly unpopular Shah. He received "billions of dollars' worth of U.S.-supplied ships, fighter aircraft, helicopters and artillery" (Hartung 1994:82). Incidentally, this advanced weaponry was inherited by the succeeding regime, to the great concern of the Pentagon (Hartung 1994). Second, the connection to the Shah made it easy for the United States to be cast in the role of the villain by those opposed to the Shah. Thus the U.S. intervention of fifty years ago has bought a staunch enemy rather than a long-term ally. The opposition of the current Iranian regime to the United States has been detrimental to long-term U.S. interests in the region. As one scholar concludes: "the fall of the shah's regime and the subsequent hostage crisis seriously undermined U.S. prestige and influence in the Middle East, making it more difficult for the United States to pursue its regional interests" (Gasiorowski 1991:226).

This pattern is not unique to Iran, but is observable in other interventions such as Guatemala and Somalia for the United States, and in Afghanistan for the Soviet Union. These problems with intervention result from the failure of intervening states to recognize the structural weakness of Third World states. In previous historical periods, intervention was more likely to further a state's long-term interests because the resulting regime was not only friendly, but could last long enough to reward the expectations of the intervening state. In the contemporary world, however, the newly installed government is often just as weak and prone to civil war as the government it replaces, leading to additional costs rather than benefits for the intervening state. While intervention may appear to have low initial costs compared to a full-scale military invasion, planners must also consider the long-term costs of support for a weak state, protection in future civil wars, and the potential cost of making long-lasting and bitter enemies if the groups it opposed eventually come to power.

7

The Logic of Twentieth-Century Civil Wars

CIVIL WARS of the late twentieth century are, to an extent, creatures of the international system. Although the particular grievances or triggers of the civil wars are local in origin, the magnitude and duration of the wars themselves are the product of international processes and resources. The international community encourages and sustains a population of structurally weak states. Such states are not able to effectively or equitably resolve political discontent, nor can they repress the insurgencies that grow as a consequence. In addition, the external resources from foreign powers—often flowing to both sides of a conflict—provide the final ingredient in the recipe for lengthy civil conflicts.

This focus on the influences of the international community paints a picture that departs substantially from previous studies of civil wars. Much of the existing literature is essentially "war-centric," examining the details of a particular conflict. As valuable as these case studies can be, there is an inevitable tendency to emphasize the local over the structural. Specific political actors and their identities, grievances, strategies, and negotiations naturally take center stage in war-centric accounts. A war might be set off by a particular political policy or resolved by an especially effective negotiator or brilliant military stratagem. Yet these actions exist within wider social structures that are too frequently overlooked. No matter how desperate or motivated, insur-

149

gent groups are almost never able to prosecute a war within a structurally strong state. Conversely, even fragmented groups at cross-purposes internally can realize military successes against a structurally frail state. To attribute causality solely to local actors and events seriously misrepresents the situation. The impact of local factors is fundamentally contingent on the broader structural factors that are often ignored or omitted from civil war accounts.

Structural Weakness, the Recurrence of Civil Wars, and the Logic of Resources

How does a civil war end, in a structurally weak state? Weak-state civil wars are rarely resolved in a definitive manner; the possibility of recurrence is almost always present. Conflicts may be brought to a close through mutual negotiation, when interstate allies withdraw, or when popular support for the war diminishes. But the structural conditions that make states vulnerable to lengthy civil wars tend to persist, regardless of the specific events that might have resolved a given conflict. Regimes—or the opposition groups that supplant them—are rarely able to develop the resources and political institutions that will stabilize a weak state. If anything, years of civil war will have further degraded the already weak economic and institutional capacities of the state. Small changes—a shift in popular support or the appearance of a new third-party intervener—may cause the civil war to flare up again.

Contemporary civil wars often recur, even years after their initial conclusion. This tendency is unusual from a historical standpoint. The civil wars of the nineteenth and early twentieth centuries typically ended decisively and permanently. In contrast, contemporary civil wars tend to have an intermittent quality, dying down for some years before coming to life once again. Conflicts may simmer for years at low intensity, then erupt or re-erupt into full-scale civil war. Liberia, Angola, Sri Lanka, the Sudan, and the Philippines are just a few examples of states that have experienced multiple civil wars within a relatively short span of years. In other cases, conflicts have not yet recurred, but one would be hesitant to rule out the possibility. Indeed, the only post-World War II civil wars that do not seem in danger of recurring are those that were related to the Cold War, because the international ideologies and resource flows supporting those wars have disappeared. Of course other transnational ideologies or movements might conceivably replace the communist agenda in the future. In short, weak states remain structurally vulnerable to civil war, whether a civil war has not yet broken out or whether one has just ended.

Weak states are vulnerable in many ways, but two factors have particular importance for the issue of recurrence. First, these states do not effectively control their territory and borders. Consequently, when their civil wars end, the losing side may not completely capitulate or be entirely defeated. Instead, the losers often retreat to the safety of marginal areas where the government has little influence or control, or take refuge in neighboring countries. The "end" of a civil war might merely mean that the insurgents were pushed into hills, mountains, or rural areas without actually surrendering. Or a regime may be toppled, but loyalists will flee across a border to rebuild their strength. Conflict diminishes to occasional attacks on locals or on government troops, but is not completely eradicated. Substantial government capacity would be needed to fully extinguish such conflicts.

Second, opposition groups are typically loose patchwork coalitions, with widely divergent aims. Thus it can be nearly impossible to satisfy all parties in the opposition coalition. The end of a war may be resolved by a peace settlement that placates the majority of insurgents, while radical factions or coalition members with different goals may be unsatisfied by the agreement and may continue fighting at a low level of intensity. Since weak states cannot control all their peripheral areas, even a handful of radical insurgents can hold out and build resources to continue a conflict in subsequent years.

In these conditions, conflicting parties can neither be destroyed nor fully placated. This dynamic explains one of the great puzzles of contemporary civil wars: why do parties fight so long and so intractably? From afar, it seems odd or even irrational that insurgencies continue for years or decades—even in conflicts where there is little hope of winning. Would not a rational actor have given up at some earlier point? Consequently, the media favors notions of "ethnic hatred" and similar ideas to account for the seemingly irrational persistence of many civil wars. Yet the sad truth is that these wars make their own kind of sense. Although it is true that contemporary civil wars often do not follow a standard logic of cost-benefit analyses, this outcome of chronic conflict is predictable given the patchwork and fragmented nature of insurgents. If opposition groups were tightly organized under a central command, they might behave more as unitary "rational actors," ending the conflict as soon as their demands were met or when victory seemed unlikely. The splintered and divergent nature of many opposition groups in weak states defies this assumption, however. Conflicts persist as long as some splinter group remains unsatisfied and has sufficient resources to fight on.

Thus weak-state civil wars appear to defy standard logics of cost-benefit analysis. Instead, they follow a *logic of resources.* The peripheral areas of weak states are safe for insurgents to operate in, and weak-state opposition groups typically have radical factions willing to carry on a conflict. The situation is analogous to global terrorists, who can hide out virtually indefinitely in peripheral areas of the world, preparing for new campaigns. The most important predictor of conflict, then, becomes the availability of sufficient resources to carry on war on a large scale. Those resources are not always easy to come by, and so third-party interveners play a crucial role in determining the course of weak-state wars. But the structural circumstances found in weak states are the critical factor in setting the stage for unending conflict.

If the opposition can neither be fully destroyed nor fully placated, how can wars ever truly end? Sadly, in many of the weaker states they never do. A number of countries experience perpetual low-intensity conflict. In some years, perhaps owing to a temporary military stalemate or a fragile cease-fire, casualties may be low enough to consider a war to be over. When fighting returns, we may say that war has recurred. But it might be more accurate to say that such wars never really ended.

The World Polity and the Future of Civil War

To the extent that the world polity shapes modern states and the wars they experience, then it is current and future changes in the world polity that may bring an end to lengthy civil wars. Of course, some changes in the world polity seem more plausible than others. Although decolonization and the decline of territorial wars created a world of weak states prone to civil war, the return of colonialism and territorial war can hardly be considered a solution, given the terrible nature of war and imperialism. More importantly, one cannot simply roll back the clock to the nineteenth century. A return of old-fashioned colonialism, for instance, is not only unthinkable but would likely spark even more deadly and intractable wars than the civil wars it replaces. Other changes in the world polity and international norms, such as the bolstering of weak states or alterations in the third-party interventions they experience, are both more plausible and more likely to lead to a reduction in civil wars. I discuss several possibilities and comment on how they might affect the character of future civil wars.

One possible solution to civil war would be for the international community to provide further support to bolster the regimes of weak states. International aid has certainly kept many weak states afloat that would have otherwise ceased functioning entirely. Indeed, in several cases the withdrawal of international aid has led to the collapse of "failed states" (Zartman 1995). Still, the international community has had few successes in which the structures of weak states have been permanently strengthened. Development aid has not historically produced strong states. More commonly, additional aid has served to enrich corrupt leaders and help them maintain power, rather than produce healthy economies and robust political institutions. To remedy this, development organizations now focus on a broader array of goals, including "institution building" and "rule of law." Yet the recipe for creating strong, stable states remains elusive. In the future, the international development regime may devise strategies that effectively yield strong economic and political structures. At present, however, development aid is not likely to rid the world of lengthy civil wars.

Another commonly mentioned solution to intractable civil war is secession (Kaufmann 1996; Sambanis 2002). Since opposition coalitions frequently claim that national independence is their goal, perhaps allowing self-government would provide a lasting resolution to the conflict. The international community has historically opposed secession, and hence secession attempts have usually failed. The world polity typically refuses to recognize secessionist regions, even in cases where insurgents have achieved *de facto* control over a contiguous territory. Without external recognition and the aid that comes with it, secessionist regions eventually collapse and are re-integrated, which, incidentally, demonstrates the critical importance of the international community in sustaining weak states.

In recent years the international community has shifted in the direction of recognizing and protecting secessionist regions. The world's recognition of Bosnia-Herzegovina, Croatia, and Slovenia as sovereign states was historically unusual. The UN has also taken a strong stance in protecting the secessionist regions of Kosovo and the Kurds of Iraq. Other sub-national groups, such as the indigenous peoples of Latin America, have also begun to gain status as international actors (Brysk 2000; Van Cott 2000). This historical shift towards international recognition of secessionist regions may alter the international ecology of states—allowing fragmented or disorganized states to be reconfigured so as to be more feasibly governable. Over time, this may result in more stable states and a decrease in the length of civil wars, particularly if secession were routinely to be seen as a legitimate option.

Although secession may alter the institutional ecology of states and eventually reduce the likelihood of new intractable wars, I am less optimistic that it will necessarily resolve wars that are already in progress. The notion that warring parties can be "split" is quite a simplification. Insurgents in weak state wars band in coalitions of many groups, often with quite different aims. Some may be satisfied by secession, but others may not. Moreover, opposition groups that have gained sovereignty often collapse into civil war among themselves. Dividing a state ravaged by war may simply result in two states that are even weaker, with smaller economies, fewer resources, and greater dependency on foreign aid.

A third option would be greater international attention and pressure for the reduction of low-level intervention. Historically, the international community has paid little attention to low-intensity interventions—the provision of resources, military equipment, and covert assistance—that are so widespread today. Whereas decisive intervention has been proscribed, flows of military aid and covert assistance have become routine, with devastating consequences for weak-state civil wars. Civil wars often cease or greatly diminish in intensity with the withdrawal of these interstate involvements, yet there is currently little awareness of the devastating effects of such low-level interventions, which allow wars to drag on for years and generate massive casualties.

International mobilization against low-level intervention might substantially reduce the length and bloodiness of civil wars. For instance, the international social movement against the use of land mines, spearheaded by Princess Diana, has led to international treaties banning the use of these destructive weapons. Greater international monitoring and attention to the milder forms of interstate participation might lead to a similar reduction in low-intensity forms of such intervention, resulting in the slowing or dissipating of weak-state civil wars.

An even more promising possibility would be the return of decisive external interventions. Traditionally, international law has regarded civil wars as purely a matter for sovereign states, over which the international community had no jurisdiction (Brownlie 1963). This tendency was reinforced during the Cold War, when international bodies such as the United Nations were careful to give the appearance of neutrality for fear of endorsing either the Western or communist model of the state. This wariness resulted in peacekeeping missions that explicitly did not try to terminate civil wars.

Since the end of the Cold War, however, the world polity has showed increasing willingness to intervene decisively in the civil conflicts and governance of other sovereign nations. The recent interventions in the civil wars in Bosnia-Herzegovina and Kosovo, for example, were reminiscent of the nineteenth century, when the European Great Powers would jointly agree on the affairs of other countries and decisively intervene to make it so. If the international community would routinely insist on the termination of civil wars in weak states, and back up its insistence with both words and actions, this would prove a powerful impetus for the ending of civil wars.

Consideration of the international dimension is essential for both academics and policymakers fully to understand the dynamics of contemporary civil wars. The assumption that civil wars are necessarily rooted in local issues, based on local resources, and fought by local combatants, has made the intractability of civil wars inexplicable, encouraging explanations that focus on the identities and local characteristics of the combatants. Once scholars begin to question the assumption that civil wars are purely domestic, however, an important piece in the puzzle of contemporary civil wars fits into place. Moreover, it is clear that in order for the world to be rid of endemic lengthy civil wars, it will take changes in the international system—not just smarter leaders or better negotiators—to bring it about.

Appendix: Data and Methods for Statistical Models

THIS APPENDIX PROVIDES information about the data sources and statistical methods used in the analyses presented in Chapter 2. Three different sets of analyses are discussed. The first set of analyses tests the institutional ecology arguments by examining global trends in civil war. Each year from 1816 to 1997 represents a separate case. In these analyses, the dependent variable is the number of civil wars occurring in the world in any given historical year, which is modeled using negative binomial regression.

The second set of analyses examines the nation-level arguments about weak states and ethnic conflict. The unit of analysis is the country-year, which is modeled using event history analysis. The object of these analyses is to determine the effect of state strength on the incidence of civil war, controlling for relevant factors. Thus all nation-states are included in the analysis from the time of their independence, not only those countries that are experiencing civil wars.

The third set of analyses examines the effects of the Cold War and interstate intervention on civil wars. In these analyses, the civil war is the unit of analysis, and the duration of each war is modeled using event-history analysis. These models examine the effects of the Cold War, superpower intervention, and other interstate intervention on the duration of civil wars.

157

Data

Civil Wars

Each type of analysis examines a different aspect of civil wars, ranging from the number ongoing in the world to the length of each one. The data on civil wars is taken from the Correlates of War dataset (Sarkees 2000; Small and Singer 1982; see Chapter 2). Dependent variables of the analyses are coded as follows.

The first set of analyses uses negative binomial regression. The dependent variable is coded as the number of ongoing civil wars occurring in the world in each year, from 1816 to 1997. (A smoothed, decadal average of this variable can be found in Figure 1.1. in Chapter 1) The data structure is a world-level time series.

Second, event-history analysis is used to model the occurrence of civil wars in historical time for each nation-state. A state is coded as having an "event" if it experiences a civil war in a given year.[1] If the civil war lasts for two years, the subsequent country-year will also be coded as having an event. This data structure was chosen in order to assess the overall level of civil war activity in a nation, resulting either from multiple short wars or single long ones. For this purpose, it would be insufficient to examine only the "event" of the onset of a new civil war. Also, it would be insufficient to examine only the length of civil wars that occurred, as this approach would not permit examination of those states that did not have any civil wars at all.

The third approach uses event-history analysis to model the duration of civil wars. The dependent variable is the number of days the war lasts.[2] Wars that had not ended by 1997 are considered right-censored.

Independent variables used in the analyses are coded in the following manner.

---

1. In cases where a state is listed in the Correlates of War as having two simultaneous civil wars in a given year, the state was coded as having a single "event" in that year.

2. For the great majority of wars the dataset provides clear criteria for war duration. However, multiple estimates are provided for a few wars. The Sarkees (2000) version of the Correlates of War provides data on upper- and lower-bound estimates of war duration. In those few cases where there was uncertainty, I took the average of the upper and lower duration estimates.

World Polity Indicators

Ex-Colonial States. The variable reflects the percentage of independent states that were formerly colonies. This variable begins near zero in 1816, when very few independent states had ever experienced colonization. The variable increases to over 60 percent following the rapid wave of decolonization in the 1960s. Colonial status of a country is defined as its having been assigned a colonial governor, based on data from Henige (1970), and was updated using data from Banks (2001). The denominator, the number of states in the world, comes from Banks (2001).

Interstate War. The measure of interstate war used in this analysis is the cumulative number of ongoing interstate wars in the world for the five years preceding any given year. The variable is intended as a general measure of the abundance or paucity of interstate war in the world at any given time. (I do not suggest any tight causal link between particular interstate wars and the onset of subsequent civil wars.) Thus the measure of interstate war is cumulated for the five years previous, to give a sense of the general prevalence. Data on interstate wars comes from the Correlates of War dataset, and includes wars defined as "interstate" war and "extra-systemic" war.

Anti-Secession Pressures. By the late twentieth century, a strong consensus had developed among states, international organizations, and scholars of international law that no international right of a region to secede should be recognized in the international community (Hannum 1996; Cassese 1995). This international anti-secession consensus developed over the course of the twentieth century. The first major anti-secession declaration is usually considered to have been the Fourteen Points speech given by Woodrow Wilson in 1914. International lawyers have also interpreted the Charter of the United Nations and other specific declarations as giving rights of self-determination to colonies but not to dissident regions that are not colonies. The measure consists of the total number of anti-secessionist declarations made by leaders and international organizations in the world polity. The list of major declarations comes from Hannum (1996).

Indicators of State Strength/Weakness

Economic and Military Capability. One aspect of state weakness is the absence of sufficient economic and military resources to build a stable state. This is commonly measured by Gross Domestic Product (GDP) per capita. Reliable GDP data for a large number of countries is available only after 1950 (Summers and Heston 1991). For analyses prior to 1945, additional measures are needed. Previous studies of the effects of economic and military capability on wars before 1945 have used data from the National Military Capabilities Dataset (Singer and Small 1999). This dataset provides measures on (a) iron and steel production, which provide necessary resources for fighting wars; (b) size of state military expenditures; and (c) number of military personnel.

The measure of economic and military capability used in the analyses in this book is constructed out of the three measures from the National Military Capabilities Dataset (NMCD) and GDP per capita. For the years 1816–1949, the three NMCD indicators (iron and steel consumption, military expenditures, and military personnel) are logged and then combined into a single index using factor analysis. From 1950 onward, GDP per capita data from the Penn World Tables is available for many countries. For 1950 to 1997, GDP per capita (logged) is also included in the factor with the other three NMCD variables in the index. Including GDP per capita helps to capture the postindustrial effect of the late twentieth century, when iron and steel production declined in many highly industrialized countries but other forms of economic activity increased. Where necessary, the data has been interpolated in order to cover gaps. If this was not possible, nation-years were omitted from the analysis.

Institutional Structure. A second aspect of state weakness is the inability of the government to supply basic services that are regarded as necessary functions of the state. There is no standard way of measuring this concept in the literature (Migdal 2001). Of the many possible indicators of government capability, I focus on measures of basic government services and capacity because they are available for a large number of states in the years preceding 1945.

The first measure of institutional structure is based on three indicators of governmental capacity: (a) the effectiveness of the legislature; (b) the number of primary and secondary school enrollments pcr capita; and (c) the amount of railroad track in a country per square mile, logged. Data on legislative effectiveness comes from the Polity IV dataset and is measured on a scale of 0 (no legislature) to 3 (effective legislature) (Marshall and Jaggers 2000). The indicators of school enrollment and railroad track are meant to measure the extent to which the government provides essential services such as education and transportation for its population. Primary and secondary school enrollment per capita and railroad track per square mile come from Banks (2001).

The strength of institutional structure can also be indirectly measured by the historical period in which the state became independent. States that became independent before 1816 were created during a period of frequent interstate and civil warfare in Europe. These states typically developed substantial infrastructures and capabilities that were required for fighting these wars. In contrast, states that became independent after 1945 were created during a period in which interstate warfare was rare and even wars of independence were unusual. These latter states may be expected to have less developed infrastructures. A dummy variable was constructed to indicate recently independent states (1 = post-1945 independence). Data on the year of independence comes from Banks (2001).

Ethnic Diversity

The propensity of ethnic groups to manifest conflict has been a difficult concept to measure quantitatively. Scholars have examined the histories of the ethnic groups and devised explanations once an ethnic conflict has broken out, as exemplified by the Minorities at Risk dataset, which provides a comprehensive list of all politically active ethnic or minority groups in the world (Gurr et al. 2002). This and other datasets do not include ethnic or minority groups that have yet to engage in ethnic conflict. This biases the data by selecting on the dependent variable: one cannot compare ethnic groups involved in political conflict with ethnic groups that have not had conflict, as there is no data on the latter group.

The few studies that have attempted to examine the rates or duration of ethnic compared to nonethnic conflict have typically used a measure of ethnic diversity as an indicator of the potential for ethnic conflict in

a given country. These researchers posit that the greater the ethnic heterogeneity of a country, the more likely it is that conflict will occur
(Sambanis 2001). Following in this tradition, I employ a measure of
ethno-linguistic diversity. This data comes from Taylor and Hudson,
and is available for only one point in time (1973). Although it seems
reasonable to assume that the ethnic diversity of a country would be
relatively constant over short periods of time (in this case, 1945 to
1997), results should be interpreted with caution. Ethno-linguistic diversity is measured on a scale from 0 to 100, with 100 indicating the
maximum amount of ethnic and linguistic diversity. Countries that
were not included in the Taylor and Hudson dataset were dropped
from these analyses.[3]

Cold War Conflicts

It is no simple task to determine which civil wars were part of the Cold
War. I have relied on multiple sources to determine those civil wars
that were considered part of the Cold War by international observers
and participants. In several cases international observers considered
a civil war to be relevant to the Cold War, although pro-Marxist or
pro-Western issues had not figured in the initial development of the
conflict. It is debatable, therefore, whether the definition of a Cold
War conflict should be based on the perceptions of local actors or of
international actors. Since international observers played such a critical role in lengthening civil wars they perceived as part of the Cold
War, regardless of local perceptions, I base the definition of a Cold
War civil war on the generally understood perceptions of the world
community.

I rely upon information from multiple sources to identify which civil
wars were influenced by the Cold War. To be coded as a Cold War civil
war, communism had to be mentioned as an aspect of the conflict in at
least two out of four comprehensive sources on civil wars: Brogan
(1998); Bercovitch and Jackson (1997); Arnold (1995); and Clodfelter
(1992). A civil war might be either pro-communist, as the civil war in
El Salvador, or anti-communist, as the U.S. backed insurgency against

---

3. The results of the analyses remained substantially similar if the mean value of ethno-linguistic diversity was substituted for countries that did not have data.

the Sandinista government in Nicaragua. A dummy variable was constructed (1 = Cold War civil war) as an indicator of these Cold War conflicts. Civil wars within a communist state that were not over communism, such as the 1967 Cultural Revolution in the People's Republic of China, were not coded as Cold War conflicts. I also constructed a post-Cold war dummy variable (1 = post-1989) to examine whether the fall of the Soviet Union and the ending of global communism had an effect on the duration of civil wars.

Intervention

Intervention is defined broadly to include armed military intervention in which foreign troops participate in the battles, as well as the provision of supplies, financing, military advisors and training, and other nonmilitary aid. The presence of intervention is indicated by the mention of such processes in any one of four comprehensive sources on civil wars: Regan (2000); Bercovitch and Jackson (1997); Arnold (1995); and Clodfelter (1992). In particular, Regan (2000) and Bercovitch and Jackson (1997) focus specifically on the occurrence of intervention in civil conflicts in this period. A dummy variable indicating intervention (1 = intervention) was coded based on the information in these four sources. Since it is difficult to get precise and reliable data, I was unable to determine more specific details consistently, such as the magnitude of the interventions or even the number of countries intervening.

I constructed variables measuring two additional aspects of intervention: whether one or both superpowers (the United States or the Soviet Union) intervened in the civil war (1 = superpower intervention), and whether intervention occurred on the side of the government and also the side of the opposition (1 = intervention on both sides) versus only one side or the other. These variables highlight important differences between interventions of the post-World War II period in comparison with interventions of earlier historical periods.

Reliable data on interventions is not available before 1945. Some data do exist, but either they are not coded according to explicit criteria (such as Leurdijk 1986), or they are limited to a very narrow definition of intervention such as having a minimum of 1,000 military personnel fighting in another country's civil war (see Small and Singer 1982). In sum, comparable data for the nineteenth century are not available for all the wars in the dataset, and so these variables are only examined in the post-1945 era.

Control Variables

For the nation-level models, I have included three variables that might reasonably be expected to affect the duration of civil wars: population size, territorial area, and level of democracy.[4] For the war-level analyses I included four control variables: population size, level of democracy, historical year, and the number of battle deaths, as used by Fearon (2002).

Population is included as a control variable in the nation-level and war-level statistical models. Data on population came from Banks (2001). It was logged in the analyses to reduce skewness. Short gaps in data were interpolated.

Territorial area is included as a control variable in the nation-level analyses. Data on territorial area in square miles are from Banks (2001). The variable was logged to reduce skewness. Short gaps in data were filled in by interpolation.

Democracy was included as a control variable in the nation-level and war-level analyses. Data on democracy use the "polity" measure from the Polity IV dataset (Marshall and Jaggers 2000). It is based on a 21-point scale, where −10 indicates an authoritarian system with no democracy and 10 indicates high levels of democracy. Democracy is conceptualized as having (a) high levels of competitiveness of political participation, (b) high levels of competitiveness, openness, and regulation in executive recruitment, and (c) high levels of constraint on the power of the chief executive. The democracy variable was lagged by one year in the analyses, in order to avoid causal ambiguity in the statistical analyses. Short gaps in data were filled in by interpolation.

Number of battle deaths was used as a control variable in the war-level analyses. Data come from the Correlates of War (Sarkees 2000), and are given as the number of casualties suffered by the state during the war. This figure was divided by the number of days the war was

---

4. Quantitative modeling of civil war events and duration represent a new direction in the field, and there are few prior studies (see Fearon 2002). Consequently, there is not yet strong consensus on what control variables should be included in such models.

fought, to avoid a tautological relationship with the dependent variable (because longer wars almost always have higher casualties). The variable was logged to correct for skewness.

Finally, the analyses of war duration include a control variable for the historical year when the war began, as listed in the Correlates of War Data set, in order to determine if there were additional historical trends in war duration beyond those captured by world polity measures. (Note: these analyses model the duration of the event; thus it is not tautological to include historical year as a variable in the analysis.)

Methods

Three different statistical approaches are used in the following analyses. The first set employs negative binomial regression to model the number of civil wars occurring in the world in each year. These analyses test the world polity hypotheses on the increased number of ongoing civil wars. Negative binomial regression is a nonlinear regression model appropriate for analyzing dependent variables that are "counts" (in other words, nonnegative integers), such as the number of civil wars occurring in the world in a given year.[5] Since all variables are conceptualized and measured as properties of the world at different points in time, this is often referred to as a "world-level" model, as opposed to nation-level or war-level models.

All other analyses employ event-history analysis. The second set of models analyzes the rate of civil-war-years among nation-states. These models test for differences in the rates of civil war for weak versus strong states by incorporating variables that measure a state's level of capabilities and institutional structure. The third set of analyses also utilizes event history to examine the characteristics of civil wars, in order to determine factors affecting the rate at which wars are resolved, given that war has broken out. These analyses focus on the effects of the Cold War and third-party intervention on the length of civil wars.

Event-history analysis examines the rate at which events happen, in contrast to regression, which looks at the magnitude of a continuous

5. Poisson models, a variant of negative binomial regression, would have been inappropriate to use because the dependent variable exhibits overdispersion, violating an important model assumption.

variable (Tuma and Hannan 1984). Event-history analysis is useful for modeling incidents or events that occur at specific points in time, such as the initiation or the termination of a civil war. Event-history models are quite flexible and can accommodate different methods of conceptualizing and operationalizing time and the occurrence of events. For instance, the nation-level analyses examine events that countries experience through historical time, while the analyses of civil war duration begin counting time with the onset of a civil war.

The nation-level analyses examine the rate of civil war years from 1816 to 1997. Countries are conceptualized as being "at risk" of having the event of civil war in each year they exist as an independent state. Countries enter the analysis, or the risk set, in the year in which they become independent. Countries that cease to exist—such as Bavaria or Saxony—drop out of the analysis when they cease to exist as states (based on data from the Correlates of War). I employ a constant rate ("exponential") event history model. Variation in the rate of wars is assumed to be a product of changing covariates, rather than of some inexorable trend over historical time.[6]

The third set of models also utilizes event-history analysis, focusing on the effects of the Cold War and interstate intervention on the duration of a civil war once it has already begun. Cases in the risk set are all civil wars that were fought from 1945 to 1997. The dependent variable is the number of days that the civil war lasts, and the hazard rate is the rate at which wars are resolved over time. All civil war cases begin at time "zero" and then continue for a number of days—whether it is tens, hundreds, or thousands of days. Thus zero is the "starting point" regardless of the historical year in which wars were initiated. I employ a Weibull event-history model with robust standard errors, which assumes a time-dependence of the hazard rate that is common among duration processes (Bennet 1999; Bennet and Stam 1996).

Results

This appendix provides more detailed statistical results than the tables presented in Chapter 2, which included only the general size of effects.

---

6. This assumption is commonly used in historical-time event history models. See Meyer et al. (1997) for an example.

The tables below present parameter coefficients, standard errors, and levels of statistical significance. See below for information about interpreting these coefficients, which are somewhat different from ordinary regression coefficients.

World-Level Analyses

The first set of analyses examines the effect of the world polity and the changing international ecology of states on the number of ongoing civil wars in the world, using negative binomial regression. Negative binomial coefficients may be interpreted by exponentiation, which yields the multiplier effect on the dependent variable for each unit-change of the independent variable. Table A.1 presents the parameter coefficients and standard errors from which the multiplier can be calculated. Results presented in Chapter 2, Table 2.1, are further simplified by converting the multiplier to an actual percentage change in the dependent variable resulting from each one-point change in an independent variable. This conversion is done simply by subtracting 1 from the multiplier (e.g., a multiplier of 1.5 corresponds to a 50 percent increase in the dependent variable).

The increasing number of ex-colonial states as a percentage of states is shown in Table A.1 to have a positive and significant effect on the number of civil wars ongoing in the world. The coefficient of .05, when

Table A.1 Negative binomial regression model: The effects of decolonization, interstate war, and anti-secession discourse on the occurrence of civil war, 1816–1997

Variables	Model 1
Ex-colonial states (as percent of all states*100)	0.05***
	(0.01)
Recent interstate war (ongoing interstate wars in past 5 years)	−0.02***
	(0.004)
International anti-secessionist declarations	0.09***
	(0.02)
Constant	−1.02***
	(0.24)
Chi-squared	252.80***

Parameter estimates and standard errors (in parentheses)
***$p<.01$, **$p<.05$, *$p<.10$, two-tailed test

exponentiated, results in a multiplier of roughly 1.05. In other words, each increase of 1 percent of states that were former colonies results in a 5 percent increase in ongoing civil wars, net of other factors. For instance, in 1945, 44 percent of the states of the world were former colonies, compared to 64 percent by 1997. As mentioned in Chapter 2, this twenty-point change would be expected to produce a 165 percent increase in the number of ongoing civil wars in the world, controlling for other factors.

The historical occurrence of interstate war has a negative and significant effect on the number of ongoing civil wars in the world. Interstate wars are measured as the cumulative number of ongoing interstate war-years that occurred in the previous five years. In 1945, for instance, there had been a total of 13 war-years of interstate wars in the previous five years (in which, for example, each year of World War II counted as one war-year), while in 1997 there had been no interstate wars at all in the past five years, according to the Correlates of War dataset. Statistical results suggest that this decline in interstate war is predicted to yield a 30 percent increase in the number of civil wars in the world from 1945 to 1997, net of other factors.

The solidification of an international consensus against secession also had a positive and significant effect on the number of ongoing civil wars. For instance, in 1945, there had been 3 international anti-secessionist declarations; while by 1997 there had been 11. Given a multiplier of 1.10, this 8-point increase in anti-secessionist discourse is estimated to have increased the number of civil wars by 114 percent, net of other factors.

Nation-level Analyses

The models presented in Tables A.2, A.3, and A.4 focus on countries as the unit of analysis and examine the rate of civil war activity in historical time. The event analyzed is the occurrence of civil war in a given year for a given country. Since the arguments of this book are concerned with the duration and recurrence of civil wars in weak states, coding the occurrence of each year of a civil war is more appropriate than modeling only the initiation of a new civil war. The units of analysis are independent nation-states. The dependent variable may be understood loosely as the rate at which independent countries experience

Table A.2 Hazard rate model: The effects of state strength on civil war years, 1945–1997

Variables	Model 2
Economic and military capability	−0.45***
	(0.11)
Governmental capacity	−0.65***
	(0.07)
Post–1945 independence	0.23*
	(0.12)
Population, logged	0.58***
	(0.06)
Territorial area, logged	0.12***
	(0.04)
Democracy	0.04***
	(0.01)
Constant	−8.76***
	(0.52)
Chi-squared	293.73***

Parameter estimates and standard errors (in parentheses).
***$p<.01$, **$p<.05$, *$p<.10$, two-tailed test.

civil wars in a given year. More precisely, the hazard rate specifies the instantaneous rate of the occurrence of a civil war year for a country, given the set of countries at risk of having civil war (Tuma and Hannan 1984).

Coefficients in event-history analysis are conventionally transformed into a hazard ratio, which is easier to interpret. The hazard ratio is simply an exponentiated version of the coefficient and represents the multiplicative effect of the variable on the hazard rate. Thus a hazard ratio of 1.0 indicates that a variable has no effect upon the dependent variables. A hazard ratio greater than 1.0 indicates that an independent variable has a positive effect on the dependent variable (for example, the rate of civil war years); a hazard ratio less than one indicates that a variable has a negative effect. The hazard ratios provide the basis for the effects presented in the tables in Chapter 2. The tables in the appendix present the parameter coefficients that provide the basis for calculating the hazard ratios, as well as the standard error and level of significance for each coefficient.

Table A.2 presents the effects of the independent variables upon the rate of civil war years from 1945 to 1997. Economic and military capability is shown to have a negative and significant effect, implying that the greater a state's capability, the lower its rate of civil war years. The institutional capacity of the state is also shown to have a negative and significant effect, indicating that states with greater governmental effectiveness have a lower rate of civil war years, controlling for other factors. The effect of governmental capacity is particularly large, with a coefficient of −.65 and a hazard ratio of .52. For each point of increased governmental capacity, a country's rate of civil war drops roughly in half. Finally, states that became independent after 1945 have a significantly higher rate of civil war years, compared to states that became independent earlier. Table A.2 provides support for the argument that states weak in economic/military capability and in institutional structure will be more prone to having lengthy civil wars (in other words, a higher rate of civil war years) than states that are stronger on these dimensions.[7]

Table A.3 compares the effects of state strength on the rate of civil war years in different historical periods. I employ a piecewise event-history model to compute coefficient effects for different historical eras. The effect of economic and military capacity varies across historical periods. Prior to 1945, the effect is positive—stronger states experienced more civil war. However, the effect is not significant in those periods. After 1945, the effect of economic and military capability is negative and statistically significant, indicating that stronger states experience a lower rate of civil war years. These models show that the effects of economic and military strength are more consequential in the recent period. The effect of government institutional capacity, in contrast, is associated with lower rates of civil war in all periods.

Table A.4 examines the effects of national ethnic diversity on the rate of civil warfare in the post–World War II period. Model 6 shows that, by itself, ethnic diversity has a strong positive effect upon the rate of civil war years. But when the indicators of state strength are added in

---

7. The positive effect of democracy in Table A.2 and elsewhere, indicating that democratic states have a higher rate of civil war-years than less democratic states, may seem surprising. The reader should note that the effect of democracy is net of the effect of economic and military capability, governmental capacity, and other variables in the model. Clearly, civil war is not common among the industrialized Western democracies. It may be the case that among the poorer and weaker states of the world, democracies are somewhat more prone to conflict. Alternately, the effect may be merely an artifact of the relatively high correlation between democracy and other state capacity measures used in the statistical analysis.

Table A.3 Hazard rate model: the effects of state strength in different historical periods on civil war years, 1816–1997

Historical period Variables	Model 3 1816–1899	Model 4 1900–1944	Model 5 1945–1997
Economic and military capability	0.44	0.04	−0.45***
	(0.28)	(0.31)	(0.11)
Governmental capacity	−0.99***	−0.93***	−0.65***
	(0.12)	(0.24)	(0.07)
Post–1945 independence	—	—	0.23*
			(0.12)
Population, logged	−0.01	0.34**	0.58***
	(0.14)	(0.15)	(0.06)
Territorial area, logged	0.43***	0.25**	0.12***
	(0.06)	(0.10)	(0.04)
Democracy	0.07***	0.03	0.04***
	(0.02)	(0.03)	(0.01)
Constant	−5.53***	−7.96***	−8.76***
	(1.30)	(1.29)	(0.52)
Chi-squared	169.96***	67.54***	293.73***

Parameter estimates and standard errors (in parentheses).
***$p<.01$, **$p<.05$, *$p<.10$, two-tailed test.

Model 7, the ethnic diversity variable ceases to be statistically significant. This suggests that ethnic diversity is a less good predictor of civil war years than the other variables added to the model—namely, measures of state strength.

War-level Analyses

Models in Tables A.5 and A.6 examine the length of civil wars. Rather than looking at nations, these event-history models look solely at wars. The event being analyzed is the *ending* of a civil war. The dependent variable is the rate at which civil wars end. Models will identify the factors that make wars last longer or bring them to a swifter conclusion. Because time is conceptualized here as the rate of war *resolution* (rather than a rate of *war*), the interpretation of the results is radically different from the previous analyses. In models of war duration, a negative parameter coefficient implies that the variable *lowers* the rate at which civil wars end, *decreasing* the rate of war termination. This is in contrast to previous models, in which factors that had positive effects were

Table A.4 Hazard rate model: The effects of ethnic diversity on civil war years, 1945–1997

Variables	Model 6	Model 7
Military capability	—	−0.26**
		(0.12)
Governmental capacity	—	−0.66***
		(0.07)
Post–1945 independence	—	0.24**
		(0.12)
Ethno-linguistic diversity	0.01***	0.003
	(0.002)	(0.002)
Population, logged	0.22***	0.48***
	(0.03)	(0.06)
Territorial area, logged	0.09***	0.13***
	(0.03)	(0.04)
Democracy	−0.03***	0.03***
	(0.01)	(0.01)
Constant	−5.64***	−8.09***
	(0.30)	(0.55)
Chi-squared	167.40***	288.84***

Parameter estimates and standard errors (in parentheses).
***$p<.01$, **$p<.05$, *$p<.10$, two-tailed test

those that *reduced* civil war activity. Thus the interpretation of effects is inverted compared to prior analyses.[8]

Table A.5 shows that the "Cold War civil war" variable has a negative effect on the rate at which wars are resolved. Cold War civil wars have a lower rate of termination, and thus typically have longer duration than civil wars not linked to the Cold War. In previous analyses, a negative effect translated to shorter civil war, but here a negative effect means

8. The numbers presented in Table 2.5 in Chapter 2 were inverted in order to give the reader a more intuitive interpretation. For example, the coefficient of the Cold War civil war variable in Model 8 is −0.88, which corresponds to a hazard ratio of .42. Subtracting 1 from a hazard ratio and multiplying by 100, which equals −58, provides a sense of the percentage impact of any one-point change of the independent variable on the dependent variable. The coefficient is properly interpreted as a 58 percent reduction in the rate of termination for Cold War civil wars. However, it is more useful to think in terms of the opposite: factors that *increase* the length of a civil war, rather than those that "reduce the rate of termination." Effects on the length of wars can be achieved by inverting the hazard ratio. Inverting the hazard ratio of .42 yields 2.41. Finally, subtracting 1.0 and multiplying by 100 results in an effect of 141 percent. This highly intuitive value, shown in Table 2.5, indicates that Cold War civil wars tend to last 141 percent longer than other types of civil wars.

Table A.5 Hazard rate model: the effects of the cold war on the duration of civil wars, 1945–1997

Variables	Model 8	Model 9
Cold War civil war	−0.88***	−0.54**
	(0.26)	(0.24)
Post–Cold war years	2.45***	2.48***
	(0.33)	(0.32)
Superpower intervention	—	−0.88***
		(0.25)
Population, logged	−0.20***	−0.24***
	(0.07)	(0.07)
Democracy, lagged	0.03	0.04**
	(0.02)	(0.02)
Historical year	−0.02**	−0.03***
	(0.01)	(0.01)
Battle deaths/year, logged	0.27***	0.28***
	(0.06)	(0.06)
Constant	43.06**	57.04***
	(19.19)	(16.52)
Chi-squared	70.61***	94.26***

Parameter estimates and robust standard errors (in parentheses).
***$p<.01$, **$p<.05$, *$p<.10$, two-tailed test.

civil wars are prolonged. Care must be taken in applying the correct interpretation to each analysis. Finally, civil wars in the post-Cold War years had a higher rate of war termination, and thus tended to be shorter, as indicated by the positive and significant effect of the post-Cold War year variable.

Moreover, the effect of the Cold War label is not reducible to superpower intervention alone. Table A.5 shows that superpower intervention has a negative and significant effect on the rate of war termination (leading to longer civil wars). However, the Cold War civil war variable remains significant, even controlling for superpower intervention. This suggests that superpower intervention was not the only factor lengthening those conflicts. Other factors, such as the strong ideological motivations associated with communism and anti-communist forces, may also have played a role in sustaining those conflicts.

Table A.6 presents the effects of interstate intervention on the duration of civil wars. Civil wars that involve a third-party intervention are significantly longer than civil wars without intervention. This effect appears in all models of Table A.6, even after variables for dual-sided

Table A.6 Hazard rate model: The effects of interstate intervention on the duration of civil wars, 1945–1997

Variables	Model 10	Model 11	Model 12
Intervention	−1.38***	−0.94***	−0.65**
	(0.27)	(0.32)	(0.32)
Intervention on both sides	—	−0.65**	−0.65**
		(0.29)	(0.27)
Superpower intervention	—	—	−0.55**
			(0.25)
Population, logged	−0.28***	−0.29***	−0.31***
	(0.07)	(0.08)	(0.08)
Democracy, lagged	0.03	0.03	0.03*
	(0.02)	(0.02)	(0.02)
Historical year	−0.02***	−0.02***	−0.03***
	(0.01)	(0.01)	(0.01)
Battle deaths/year	0.30***	0.30***	0.30***
	(0.07)	(0.07)	(0.07)
Constant	44.37***	40.44**	48.87***
	(14.81)	(16.29)	(15.69)
Chi-squared	41.48***	37.19***	51.70***

Parameter estimates and robust standard errors (in parentheses).
***$p<.01$, **$p<.05$, *$p<.10$, two-tailed test

intervention and superpower intervention are added to the model. Furthermore, civil wars in which there is intervention on both sides and/or in which there is superpower intervention tend to last even longer. All effects in this model are extremely large. Alone, each factor in Model 12—intervention, dual-sided intervention, and superpower intervention—has a hazard ratio in the area of 0.5, lowering the rate of war resolution by over half. The combined effect of intervention on both sides and superpower intervention slows the rate of resolution by 84 percent, effectively lengthening the typical war by over 5 times. In sum, interstate interventions of any kind drastically increase the length of civil wars.

THE ANALYSES presented above represent three different lenses on civil war. The first set of analyses looks from a distance at the global trends which affect the overall incidence of civil wars in the world. Factors encouraging the proliferation of weak states—such as decolonization—increase the overall level of civil wars in the world. Second, national attributes, most notably the strength of the state, determine whether a given country experiences a great deal of civil war activity. Finally, once a war has begun, I find that intervention and connection to the Cold War play a major role in increasing the duration of civil wars. Previous chapters examined these processes in greater detail.

References

Abracosa, Ramon, and Leonard Ortolano. "Environmental Impact Assessment in the Philippines, 1977–1985." *EIA Review.* 7(4):293–310, 1987.

Adam, Hussein M. "Somalia: A Terrible Beauty Being Born?" Pp. 69–90 in I. William Zartman (ed.) *Collapsed States: The Disintegration and Restoration of Legitimate Authority.* Boulder: Lynne Rienner, 1995.

Anderson, G. Norman. *Sudan in Crisis: The Failure of Democracy.* Gainesville: University Press of Florida, 1999.

Ardant, Gabriel. "Financial Policy and Economic Infrastructure of Modern States and Nations." Pp. 164–242 in Charles Tilly (ed.), *The Formation of National States in Western Europe.* Princeton: Princeton University Press, 1975.

Arnold, G. L. *The Pattern of World Conflict.* New York: Dial Press, 1955.

Arnold, Guy. *Wars in the Third World since 1945.* New York: Cassell, 1995.

Attalides, Michael A. *Cyprus: Nationalism and International Politics.* New York: St. Martin's Press, 1979.

Badie, Bertrand, *The Imported State: The Westernization of the Political Order.* Stanford: Stanford University Press, 2000.

Badie, Bertrand, and Pierre Birnbaum. *The Sociology of the State,* trans. Arthur Goldhammer. Chicago: University of Chicago Press, 1983.

Banks, Arthur. S. *Cross-National Time-Series Data Archive (dataset).* Binghamton, NY: Computer Systems Unlimited, 2001.

Barnet, Richard J. *Intervention and Revolution.* Cleveland: World Publishing Company, 1968.

Barth, Fredrik (ed). *Ethnic Groups and Boundaries.* Boston: Little, Brown, 1969.

Bendix, Reinhard. *Kings or People: Power and the Mandate to Rule.* Berkeley: University of California Press, 1978.

——— *Nation-Building and Citizenship.* New York: John Wiley, 1964.

Bennet, D. Scott. "Parametric Models, Duration Dependence, and Time-varying Data Revisited." *American Journal of Political Science* 43:256–270, 1999.

Bennet, D. Scott, and Allan C. Stam III. "The Duration of Interstate Wars, 1816–1985." *American Political Science Review* 90:239–57, 1996.

Bercovitch, Jacob, and Richard Jackson. *International Conflict.* Washington, D.C.: Congressional Quarterly, 1997.

Berg, Ronald H. "Peasant Responses to Shining Path in Andahuaylas." Pp. 101–122 in David Scott Palmer (ed.), *The Shining Path of Peru*, 2nd ed. New York: St. Martin's Press, 1994.

Black, Jeremy. "Enduring Rivalries: Britain and France." Pp. 254–268 in William R. Thompson (ed.), *Great Power Rivalries.* Columbia: University of South Carolina Press, 1999.

Boli, John. "Sovereignty from a World Polity Perspective." Pp. 53–82 in Stephen D. Krasner (ed.), *Problematic Sovereignty.* New York: Columbia University Press, 2001.

Booth, John A., and Thomas W. Walker. *Understanding Central America*, 3rd ed. Boulder: Westview Press, 1999.

Brogan, Patrick. *World Conflicts.* Lanham, MD: Scarecrow Press, 1998.

Brownlie, Ian. *International Law and the Use of Force by States.* Oxford: Clarendon Press, 1963.

Brysk, Alison. *From Tribal Village to Global Village: Indian Rights and International Relations in Latin America.* Stanford: Stanford University Press, 2000.

Bull, Hedley. "Intervention in the Third World." Pp. 135–156 in Hedley Bull (ed.), *Intervention in World Politics.* Oxford: Clarendon Press, 1984.

Calhoun, Craig. *Nationalism.* Minneapolis: University of Minnesota Press, 2002.

Callahan, David. *Unwinnable Wars: American Power and Ethnic Conflict.* New York: Hill and Wang, 1998.

Carothers, Thomas. "The Rule of Law Revival." *Foreign Affairs.* 77:95–106, 1998.

Carre, Rene Albrecht (ed.). *The Concert of Europe.* New York: Walker, 1968.

Cassese, Antonio. *Self-Determination of Peoples: A Legal Reappraisal.* Cambridge: Cambridge University Press, 1995.

Chapman, William. *Inside the Philippine Revolution.* New York: W. W. Norton, 1987.

Che Man, W. K. *Muslim Separatism: The Moros of Southern Philippines and the Malays of Southern Thailand.* New York: Oxford University Press, 1990.

Clapham, Christopher. "Introduction: Analyzing African Insurgencies." Pp. 1–18 in Christopher Clapham (ed.), *African Guerrillas.* Bloomington: Indiana University Press, 1998.

Clodfelter, Micheal. *Warfare and Armed Conflicts: A Statistical Reference*, vols. 1–2. Jefferson, NC: McFarland, 1992.

Conant, Lisa J. *Contested Boundaries: Citizens, States and Supranational Belonging in the European Union.* San Domenico, Italy: European University Institute, 2001.

Cornell, Stephen, and Douglas Hartmann. *Ethnicity and Race: Making Identities in a Changing World.* Thousand Oaks, CA: Pine Forge Press, 1998.

Cornell, Svante E. "Autonomy as a Source of Conflict: Caucasian Conflicts in Theoretical Perspective." *World Politics* 54(2):245–276, 2002.

Cullather, Nick. *Illusions of Influence: The Political Economy of United States-Phillipines Relations, 1942–1960.* Stanford: Stanford University Press, 1994.

Damrosch, Lori Fisler (ed.). *Enforcing Restraint: Collective Intervention in Internal Conflicts.* New York: Council on Foreign Relations Press, 1993.

Darwin, John. *The End of the British Empire: The Historical Debate.* Oxford: Basil Blackwell, 1991.

Davis, Lance E., and Robert A. Huttenbeck. *Mammon and the Pursuit of Empire.* Cambridgeshire: Cambridge University Press, 1986.

Diehl, Paul F., Jennifer Reifschneider, and Paul R. Hensel. "United Nations Intervention and Recurring Conflict." *International Organization* 50(4):683–700, 1996.

Dobbin, Frank. *Forging Industrial Policy: The United States, Britain and France in the Railway Age.* New York: Cambridge University Press, 1994.

Donald, David Herbert, Jean Harvey Baker, and Michael F. Holt. *The Civil War and Reconstruction.* New York: W. W. Norton, 2001.

Dos Santos, Daniel. "Cabinda: The Politics of Oil in Angola's Enclave." Pp. 101–118 in Robin Cohen (ed.), *African Islands and Enclaves.* Beverly Hills: Sage, 1983.

Elbadawi, Ibrahim A., and Nicholas Sambanis. *External Interventions and the Duration of Civil Wars.* Washington, D.C.: The World Bank, 2000.

Eller, Jack David, and Reed M. Coughlan. "The Poverty of Primordialism." *Ethnic and Racial Studies* 16(April):183–200, 1993.

Emerson, Rupert. *From Empire to Nation: The Rise to Self-assertion of Asian and African Peoples.* Boston: Beacon Press, 1960.

Eprile, Cecil. *War and Peace in the Sudan, 1955–1972.* London: David and Charles, 1974.

Esman, Milton J., and Ronald J. Herring (eds.). *Carrots, Sticks, and Ethnic Conflict: Rethinking Development Assistance.* Ann Arbor: University of Michigan Press, 2001.

Esposito, John L. *The Islamic Threat: Myth or Reality?* 3rd ed. New York: Oxford University Press, 1999.

Fearon, James D. "Why Do Some Civil Wars Last So Much Longer than Others?" Stanford University: unpublished manuscript, 2002.

Fearon, James D., and David D. Laitin. "Ethnicity, Insurgency, and Civil War." *American Political Science Review* 97(1):1–17, 2003.

——— "Explaining Interethnic Cooperation." *American Political Science Review* 90(4):715–735, 1996.

Feste, Karen A. *Expanding the Frontiers: Superpower Intervention in the Cold War.* New York: Praeger, 1992.

Fieldhouse, David Kenneth. *Economics and Empire, 1830–1914.* Ithaca: Cornell University Press, 1973.

——— *The Colonial Empires: A Comparative Survey from the Eighteenth Century.* New York: Dell Publishing Company, 1966.

Finnemore, Martha. *National Interests in International Society.* Ithaca: Cornell University Press, 1996.

Fituni, Leonid L. "The Collapse of the Socialist State: Angola and the Soviet Union." Pp. 143–156 in I. William Zartman (ed.), *Collapsed States.* Boulder: Lynne Rienner, 1995.

Fox, Jonathan. "The Influence of Religious Legitimacy on Grievance Formation by Ethno-Religious Minorities." *Journal of Peace Research* 36(3):289–307, 1999.

Frederick, Suzanne Y. "The Anglo-German Rivalry, 1890–1914." Pp. 306–336 in William R. Thompson (ed.), *Great Power Rivalries.* Columbia: University of South Carolina Press, 1999.

Gaddis, John Lewis. *We Now Know: Rethinking Cold War History*. Oxford: Clarendon Press, 1997.

———— *Strategies of Containment: A Critical Appraisal of Postwar American National
Security Policy*. New York: Oxford University Press, 1982.

Gans, Herbert J. "Symbolic Ethnicity." Pp. 167–199 in *Making Sense of America*.
Lanham: Rowman and Littlefield, 1999.

Gantzel, Klaus Jurgen. "War in the Post-World War II World: Some Empirical
Trends and a Theoretical Approach." Pp. 123–144 in David Turton (ed.), *War
and Ethnicity: Global Connections and Local Violence*. Rochester, NY: University
of Rochester Press, 1997.

Gasiorowski, Mark J. *U.S. Foreign Policy and the Shah: Building a Client State in Iran*.
Ithaca: Cornell University Press, 1991.

Gellner, Ernest. *Nations and Nationalism*. Ithaca: Cornell University Press, 1983.

George, Alexander L., and Richard Smoke. *Deterrence in American Foreign Policy:
Theory and Practice*. New York: Columbia University Press, 1974.

Gerard-Libois, Jules. *Katanga Secession*, trans. Rebecca Young. Madison: University
of Wisconsin Press, 1966.

Gilpin, Robert. *War and Change in World Politics*. Cambridge: Cambridge University Press, 1981.

Gleijeses, Piero. *Shattered Hope: The Guatemalan Revolution and the United States,
1944–1954*. Princeton: Princeton University Press, 1991.

Goodwin, Jeff. *No Other Way Out: States and Revolutionary Movements, 1945–1991*.
New York: Cambridge University Press, 2001.

Graebner, Norman A. "Myth and Reality: America's Rhetorical Cold War."
Pp. 20–37 in Martin J. Medhurst and H. W. Brands (eds.), *Critical Reflections on
the Cold War: Linking Rhetoric and History*. College Station: Texas A&M University Press, 2000.

Grimal, Henri. *Decolonization: The British, French, Dutch and Belgian Empires, 1919–
1963*, trans. Stephan De Vos. London: Routledge and Kegan Paul, 1965.

Gurr, Ted Robert, and Barbara Harff. *Ethnic Conflict in World Politics*. Boulder:
Westview Press, 1994.

Gurr, Ted Robert, Monty G. Marshall, and Christian Davenport. *Minorities at Risk
(dataset)*. College Park: Center for International Development and Conflict
Management, 2002.

Hall, Margaret, and Tom Young. *Confronting Leviathan: Mozambique since Independence*. Athens: Ohio University Press, 1997.

Hannum, Hurst. *Autonomy, Sovereignty and Self-Determination*. Philadelphia: University of Pennsylvania Press, 1996.

Hartung, William D. *And Weapons for All*. New York: Harper Collins, 1994.

Hechter, Michael. *Containing Nationalism*. Oxford: Oxford University Press, 2000.

Henderson, Errol A. "Culture or Contiguity: Ethnic Conflict, the Similarity of
States, and the Onset of War, 1820–1989." *Journal of Conflict Resolution*
41(5):649–668, 1997.

Henige, David P. *Colonial Governors from the Fifteenth Century to the Present*. Madison: University of Wisconsin Press, 1970.

Herbst, Jeffrey. *States and Power in Africa: Comparative Lessons in Authority and Control*. Princeton: Princeton University Press, 2000.

Higgins, Rosalyn. "International Law and Civil Conflict." Pp. 169–186 in Evan

Luard (ed.), *The International Regulation of Civil Wars.* London: Thames and Hudson, 1972.

Hironaka, Ann. "Boundaries of War: Historical Changes in Types of War, 1816–1980." Ph.D. diss. Stanford University, 1998.

Hobsbawm, Eric J. *Nations and Nationalism since 1780.* New York: Cambridge University Press, 1990.

Hoffmann, Stanley. *The Ethics and Politics of Humanitarian Intervention.* Notre Dame: University of Notre Dame Press, 1996.

———"The Problem of Intervention." Pp. 7–28 in Hedley Bull (ed.), *Intervention in World Politics.* Oxford: Clarendon Press, 1984.

Holland, R. F. *European Decolonization 1918–1981: An Introductory Survey.* New York: St. Martin's Press, 1985.

Holsti, Kalevi J. *The State, War, and the State of War.* Cambridge: Cambridge University Press, 1996.

Horne, Alastair. *The Fall of Paris: The Siege and the Commune, 1870–1.* London: Papermac, 1989.

Horowitz, Donald L. *Ethnic Groups in Conflict.* Berkeley: University of California Press, 2000.

Huntington, Samuel P. *The Clash of Civilizations and the Remaking of World Order.* New York: Simon and Schuster, 1996.

Huth, Paul K. *Standing Your Ground: Territorial Disputes and International Conflict.* Ann Arbor: University of Michigan Press, 1996.

Ikle, Fred Charles. *Every War Must End.* New York: Columbia University Press, 1991.

Jackson, Robert H., *Quasi-States: Sovereignty, International Relations, and the Third World.* Cambridge: Cambridge University Press, 1990.

Jackson, Robert H., and Carl G. Rosberg. "Why Africa's Weak States Persist: The Empirical and the Juridical in Statehood." *World Politics* 35:1–24, 1982.

Jahn, George. "NATO Jets Hit Chinese Embassy in Belgrade, Dead and Wounded." Associated Press. May 8, 1999.

Jentleson, Bruce W., Ariel E. Levite, and Larry Berman. "Foreign Military Intervention in Perspective." Pp. 301–326 in Ariel E. Levite, Bruce W. Jentleson, and Larry Berman (eds.). *Foreign Military Intervention: The Dynamics of Protracted Conflict.* New York: Columbia University Press, 1992.

Jepperson, Ronald L. "The Development and Application of Sociological Neo-institutionalism." Badia Fiesolana, San Domenico: EUI Working Paper RSC No. 2001/5, 2001.

Jepperson, Ronald L., Alexander Wendt, and Peter J. Katzenstein. "Norms, Identity, and Culture in National Security." Pp. 33–75 in Peter J. Katzenstein (ed.), *The Culture of National Security.* New York: Columbia University Press, 1996.

Joes, Anthony James. *America and Guerrilla Warfare.* Lexington: University Press of Kentucky, 2000.

Johnston, Alexander. "Ethnic Conflict in Post Cold War Africa: Four Case Studies (Rwanda, Liberia, Somalia and Kwazulu-Natal)." Pp. 129–152 in Kenneth Christie (ed.), *Ethnic Conflict, Tribal Politics.* Richmond, Surrey: Curzon Press, 1998.

Jones, Gregg R. *Red Revolution: Inside the Philippine Guerrilla Movement.* Boulder: Westview Press, 1989.

Kahin, George McT. *Intervention: How America Became Involved in Vietnam.* New York: Anchor, 1986.

Kaldor, Mary. *New and Old Wars: Organized Violence in a Global Era.* Stanford: Stanford University Press, 1999.

Kaplan, Robert. "History's Cauldron." *Atlantic Monthly* (June): 92–104, 1991.

Kaufmann, Chaim. "Possible and Impossible Solutions to Ethnic Civil Wars." *International Security* 20(4):136–175, 1996.

Kennedy-Pipe, Caroline. *The Origins of the Present Troubles in Northern Ireland.* New York: Longman, 1997.

Kessler, Richard J. *Rebellion and Repression in the Philippines.* New Haven: Yale University Press, 1989.

Kirkpatrick, Jeanne. "Dictatorships and Double Standards." *Commentary* 68:34–45, 1997.

Krasner, Stephen D. *Sovereignty: Organized Hypocrisy.* Princeton: Princeton University Press, 1999.

Kunovich, Robert M., and Randy Hodson. "Conflict, Religious Identity and Ethnic Intolerance in Croatia." *Social Forces.* 78(2):643–668, 1999.

Laitin, David D., and Said S. Samatar. *Somalia: Nation in Search of a State.* Boulder: Westview Press, 1987.

Layachi, Azzedine. "Algeria: Reinstating the State or Instating a Civil Society?" Pp. 171–190 in I. William Zartman (ed.), *Collapsed States: The Disintegration and Restoration of Legitimate Authority.* Boulder: Lynne Rienner, 1995.

Leonard, Thomas M. *Central America and the United States: The Search for Stability.* Athens: University of Georgia Press, 1991.

Leurdijk, J. H. *Intervention in International Politics.* Leeuwarden, Netherlands: Eisma B.V., 1986.

Lewis, I. M. *A Modern History of Somalia: Nation and State in the Horn of Africa.* Boulder: Westview Press, 1988.

Little, David. *Sri Lanka: The Invention of Enmity.* Washington, D.C.: U.S. Institute of Peace Press, 1994.

Lowenkopf, Martin. "Liberia: Putting the State Back Together." Pp. 91–108 in I. William Zartman (ed.), *Collapsed States: The Disintegration and Restoration of Legitimate Authority.* Boulder: Lynne Rienner, 1995.

Luard, Evan. "Civil Conflicts in Modern International Relations." Pp. 7–25 in Evan Luard (ed.), *The International Regulation of Civil Wars.* London: Thames and Hudson, 1972.

Lynch, Peter. *Minority Nationalism and European Integration.* Cardiff: University of Wales Press, 1996.

MacDonald, Douglas J. *Adventures in Chaos: American Intervention for Reform in the Third World.* Cambridge, MA: Harvard University Press, 1992.

MacFarlane, S. Neil. "Successes and Failures in Soviet Policy towards Marxist Revolutions in the Third World, 1917–1985." Pp. 6–50 in Mark N. Katz (ed.), *The USSR and Marxist Revolutions in the Third World.* Cambridge: Cambridge University Press, 1990.

MacQueen, Norrie. *The United Nations since 1945: Peacekeeping and the Cold War.* New York: Longman, 1999.

Manor, James. "'Ethnicity' and Politics in India." *International Affairs* 72(3):459–475, 1996.

March, James G., and Johan P. Olsen. "The New Institutionalism: Organizational Factors in Political Life." *American Political Science Review* 78(3):734–749, 1984.

Marks, Thomas A. *Maoist Insurgency since Vietnam*. Portland, OR: Frank Cass, 1996.

Marshall, Monty G. "Systems at Risk: Violence, Diffusion, and Disintegration in the Middle East." Pp. 82–115 in David Carment and Patrick James (eds.), *Wars in the Midst of Peace: The International Politics of Ethnic Conflict*. Pittsburgh: University of Pittsburgh Press, 1997.

Marshall, Monty G., and Jaggers, K. *Polity IV Project: Political Regime Characteristics and Transitions, 1800–1999 (dataset)*. College Park, MD: Center for International Development and Conflict Management, 2000.

Maynes, C. "Containing Ethnic Conflict." *Foreign Policy* 90 (Spring):3–21, 1993.

McNamara, Robert S., James G. Blight, and Robert K. Brigham. *Argument without End: In Search of Answers to the Vietnam Tragedy*. New York: Public Affairs, 1999.

McNeely, Connie L. *Constructing the Nation-State: International Organization and Prescriptive Action*. Westport: Greenwood Press, 1995.

Meyer, John W., John Boli, George Thomas, and Francisco O. Ramirez. "World Society and the Nation-State." *American Journal of Sociology* 103:144–81, 1997.

Meyer, Marshall W., and Lynn Zucker. *Permanently Failing Organizations*. Newberry Park, CA: Sage Publications, 1989.

Migdal, Joel. S. *State in Society: Studying How States and Societies Transform and Constitute One Another*. New York: Cambridge University Press, 2001.

—— *Strong Societies and Weak States: State-Society Relations and State Capabilities in the Third World*. Princeton: Princeton University Press, 1988.

Minahan, James. *Nations without States*. Westport: Greenwood Press, 1995.

Minter, William. *Apartheid's Contras*. Atlantic Highlands, NJ: Zed Books, 1994.

Minority Rights Group (ed.) *World Directory of Minorities*. London: Minority Rights Group International, 1990.

Montgomery, Tommie Sue. *Revolution in El Salvador, from Civil Strife to Civil Peace*, 2nd ed. Boulder: Westview Press, 1995.

Murphey, Dwight D. "The Rule of Law and Democracy." *Journal of Social, Political and Economic Studies* 24(1):93–118, 1999.

Nagel, Joane. "Constructing Ethnicity: Creating and Recreating Ethnic Identity and Culture." *Social Problems* 41:152–168, 1994.

Nettl, J. P. "The State as a Conceptual Variable." *World Politics* 20:559–92, 1968.

Newitt, Malyn. *Portugal in Africa: The Last Hundred Years*. London: C. Hurst, 1981.

Ng'ethe, Njuguna. "Strongmen, State Formation, Collapse, and Reconstruction in Africa." Pp. 251–266 in I. William Zartman (ed.), *Collapsed States: The Disintegration and Restoration of Legitimate Authority*. Boulder: Lynne Rienner, 1995.

O'Ballance, Edgar. *Sudan, Civil War and Terrorism, 1956–99*. New York: St. Martin's Press, 2000.

Odom, William E. *On Internal War: American and Soviet Approaches to Third World Clients and Insurgents*. Durham: Duke University Press, 1992.

Olzak, Susan, and Kiyoteru Tsutsui. "Status in the World System and Ethnic Mobilization." *Journal of Conflict Resolution* 42(6):691–720, 1998.

Pastor, Robert A. *Condemned to Repetition: The United States and Nicaragua*. Princeton: Princeton University Press, 1987.

Pearson, Frederick S. "Foreign Interventions and Domestic Disputes." *International Studies Quarterly* 18(3):259–289, 1974.

Phillips, Walter Alison. *The Confederation of Europe*. New York: Longmans, Green, 1920.

Poggi, Gianfranco. *The Development of the Modern State*. Stanford: Stanford University Press, 1978.

Porter, Bruce D. *The USSR in Third World Conflicts: Soviet Arms and Diplomacy in Local Wars, 1945–1980*. Cambridge: Cambridge University Press, 1984.

Putnam, Robert D. *Making Democracy Work*. Princeton: Princeton University Press, 1993.

Rabe, Stephen G. "The Clues Didn't Check Out: Commentary on 'The CIA and Castillo Armas.'" *Diplomatic History* 14(1):87–95, 1990.

Regan, Patrick M. *Civil Wars and Foreign Powers: Outside Intervention in Intrastate Conflict*. Ann Arbor: University of Michigan Press, 2000.

Richardson, Lewis Fry. *Statistics of Deadly Quarrels*. Pittsburg: Boxwood Press, 1960.

Rotberg, Robert I. "Sri Lanka's Civil War: From Mayhem toward Diplomatic Resolution." Pp. 1–16 in Robert I. Rotberg (ed.), *Creating Peace in Sri Lanka: Civil War and Reconciliation*. Washington, D.C.: Brookings Institution Press, 1999.

Rothchild, Donald, and Caroline Hartzell. "The Case of Angola: Four Power Intervention and Disengagement." Pp. 163–208 in Ariel E. Levite, Bruce W. Jentleson, and Larry Berman (eds.), *Foreign Military Intervention: The Dynamics of Protracted Conflict*. New York: Columbia University Press, 1992.

Rubin, Barry. "Islamist Movements in the Middle East." Pp. 207–218 in Barry Rubin (ed.), *Revolutionaries and Reformers: Contemporary Islamist Movements in the Middle East*. Albany: State University of New York Press, 2003.

Sadowski, Yahya. *The Myth of Global Chaos*. Washington, D.C.: Brookings Institution Press, 1998.

Saideman, Stephen M. *The Ties That Divide: Ethnic Politics, Foreign Policy, and International Conflict*. New York: Columbia University Press, 2001.

——— "Explaining the International Relations of Secessionist Conflicts." *International Organization* 51(4):721–753, 1997.

Sambanis, Nicholas. "Partition as a Solution to Ethnic War." *World Politics* 52(4):437–483, 2002.

——— "Do Ethnic and Nonethnic Civil Wars Have the Same Causes?" *Journal of Conflict Resolution* 45(3):259–282, 2001.

Sarkees, Meredith Reid. "The Correlates of War Data on War: An Update to 1997." *Conflict Management and Peace Science* 18(1):123–144, 2000.

Schattschneider, Elmer Eric. *The Semisovereign People: A Realist's View of Democracy in America*. New York: Holt, Rinehart and Winston, 1960.

Schlesinger, Stephen, and Stephen Kinzer. *Bitter Fruit: The Untold Story of the American Coup in Guatemala*. Garden City, NY: Anchor, 1982.

Schofer, Evan, and Ann Hironaka. "World Society and Environmental Protection Outcomes." *Social Forces*, forthcoming.

Seligman, Adam B. *The Idea of Civil Society*. New York: Free Press, 1992.

Shafer, D. Michael. *Deadly Paradigms: The Failure of U.S. Counterinsurgency Policy*. Princeton: Princeton University Press, 1988.

Sharlet, Robert. "Bringing the Rule of Law to Russia and the Newly Independent States: The Role of the West in the Transformation of the Post-Soviet Legal Systems." Pp. 322–349 in Karen Dawisha (ed.), *The International Dimension of*

Post-Communist Transitions in Russia and the New States of Eurasia. Armonk, NY: M. E. Sharpe, 1997.

Singer, J. David, and Melvin Small. *National Material Capabilities Dataset.* Ann Arbor, MI: Correlates of War Project, 1999.

Sislin, John, and Frederic S. Pearson. *Arms and Ethnic Conflict.* Lanham: Rowman and Littlefield, 2001.

Sivard, Ruth Leger. *World Military and Social Expenditures.* Washington, D.C.: World Priorities, 1996.

Skocpol, Theda. *States and Social Revolutions: A Comparative Analysis of France, Russia, and China.* New York: Cambridge University Press, 1979.

Skowronek, Stephen. *Building a New American State: The Expansion of National Administrative Capacities, 1877–1920.* New York: Cambridge University Press, 1982.

Small, Melvin, and J. David Singer. *Resort to Arms: International and Civil Wars, 1816–1980.* Beverly Hills: Sage, 1982.

Smith, Anthony D. *The Ethnic Revival.* Cambridge: Cambridge University Press, 1981.

Smith, Chris. "South Asia's Enduring War." Pp. 17–40 in Robert I. Rotberg (ed.), *Creating Peace in Sri Lanka: Civil War and Reconciliation.* Washington, D.C.: Brookings Institution Press, 1999.

Snow, David A., and Robert D. Benford. "Ideology, Frame Resonance and Participant Mobilization." *International Social Movement Research* 1:197–217, 1988.

Snyder, David, and Charles Tilly. 1972. "Hardship and Collective Violence in France, 1830–1960." *American Sociological Review.* 37:520–32, 1972.

Snyder, Jack L. *From Voting to Violence.* New York: W. W. Norton, 2000.

Somerville, Keith. *Foreign Military Intervention in Africa.* New York: St. Martin's Press, 1990.

Soysal, Yasemin Nuhoglu. *Limits of Citizenship: Migrants and Postnational Membership in Europe.* Chicago: University of Chicago Press, 1994.

Sperber, Jonathan. *Revolutionary Europe, 1780 1850.* New York: Longman, 2000.

Stedman, Stephen John, Donald Rothchild, and Elizabeth M. Cousens (eds.). *Ending Civil Wars: The Implementation of Peace Agreements.* Boulder: Lynne Rienner, 2002.

Strang, David. "From Dependency to Sovereignty: An Event History Analysis of Decolonization, 1870–1987." *American Sociological Review* 55(6):846–860, 1990.

Stockholm International Peace Research Institute (SIPRI). *World Armaments and Disarmaments.* New York: Humanities Press, 1995–2003.

Streeter, Stephen M. *Managing the Counterrevolution: The United States and Guatemala, 1954–1961.* Athens, OH: Ohio University Center for International Studies, 2000.

Suchman, Mark C., and Dana P. Eyre. "Military Procurement as Rational Myth: Notes on the Social Construction of Weapons Proliferation." *Sociological Forum* 7:137–61, 1992.

Summers, Robert, and Alan Heston. "The Penn World Table, Mark 5, 1950–1988." *Quarterly Journal of Economics* 2:1–41, 1991.

Taylor, Charles Lewis, and Michael C. Hudson. *World Handbook of Political and Social Indicators.* Ann Arbor: Inter-University Consortium for Political Research, 1973.

Thomas, George M., John W. Meyer, Francisco O. Ramirez, and John Boli. *Insti-*

tutional Structure: Constituting State, Society, and the Individual. Newbury Park: Sage Publications, 1987.

Thomson, Janice E. *Mercenaries, Pirates, and Sovereigns: State-building and Extraterritorial Violence in Early Modern Europe.* Princeton: Princeton University Press, 1994.

Tillema, Herbert K. *International Armed Conflict since 1945.* Boulder: Westview Press, 1991.

———— *Appeal to Force: American Military Intervention in the Era of Containment.* New York: Thomas Y. Crowell, 1973.

Tilly, Charles. *European Revolutions, 1492–1992.* Cambridge: Blackwell, 1993.

———— *Coercion, Capital and European States, AD 990–1992.* Cambridge: Blackwell, 1992.

———— "Reflection on the History of European State-Making." Pp. 3–83 in Charles Tilly (ed.), *The Formation of National States in Western Europe.* Princeton: Princeton University Press, 1975.

Tombs, Robert. *The Paris Commune, 1871.* New York: Longman, 1999.

Tuma, Nancy Brandon, and Michael T. Hannan. *Social Dynamics: Models and Methods.* Orlando: Academic Press, 1984.

United Nations. *The Blue Helmets: A Review of United Nations Peacekeeping,* 2nd ed. New York: United Nations Press, 1990.

Uyangoda, Jayadeva. "A Political Culture of Conflict." Pp. 157–168 in Robert I. Rotberg (ed.), *Creating Peace in Sri Lanka: Civil War and Reconciliation.* Washington, D.C.: Brookings Institution Press, 1999.

Van Cott, Donna Lee. *The Friendly Liquidation of the Past: The Politics of Diversity in Latin America.* Pittsburgh: University of Pittsburgh Press, 2000.

Vanhanen, Tatu. "Domestic Ethnic Conflict and Ethnic Nepotism: A Comparative Analysis." *Journal of Peace Research* 36(1):55–73, 1999.

Vincent, R. J. *Nonintervention and International Order.* Princeton: Princeton University Press, 1974.

Vines, Alex. *Renamo: Terrorism in Mozambique.* Bloomington: Indiana University Press, 1991.

Walter, Barbara F. *Committing to Peace: The Successful Settlement of Civil Wars.* Princeton: Princeton University Press, 2002.

Waltz, Kenneth N. *Theory of International Politics.* Reading, MA: Addison-Wesley, 1979.

Weber, Eugen. *Peasants into Frenchmen: The Modernization of Rural France, 1870–1914.* Stanford: Stanford University Press, 1976.

Weber, Max. *Economy and Society.* Guenther Roth and Claus Wittich (eds.). Berkeley: University of California Press, 1968.

Weisburd, A. Mark. *Use of Force: The Practice of States since World War II.* University Park: Pennsylvania State University Press, 1997.

World Bank. *World Tables of Economic and Social Indicators.* Ann Arbor: Inter-University Consortium for Political and Social Research, 2000.

Wright, Thomas C. *Latin America in the Era of the Cuban Revolution.* New York: Praeger, 1991.

Young, Crawford. *The Politics of Cultural Pluralism.* Madison: University of Wisconsin Press, 1976.

———— *Politics in the Congo: Decolonization and Independence.* Princeton: Princeton University Press, 1965.

Young, Robert A. *The Struggle for Quebec: From Referendum to Referendum?* Montreal: McGill-Queen's University Press, 1999.

Zacher, Mark W. "The Territorial Integrity Norm: International Boundaries and the Use of Force." *International Organization* 55(2):215–250, 2001.

Zartman, I. William. "Introduction: Posing the Problem of State Collapse." Pp. 1–14 in I. William Zartman (ed.), *Collapsed States: The Disintegration and Restoration of Legitimate Authority.* Boulder: Lynne Rienner, 1995.

——— "Internationalization of Communal Strife: Temptations and Opportunities of Triangulation." Pp. 27–44 in Manus I. Midlarsky (ed.), *The Internationalization of Communal Strife.* New York: Routledge, 1992.

Index

189